The Australian Family Vegetarian Cookbook

The Australian Family Vegetarian Cook Book

Quick-and-Easy, Kid-Tempting, Sugarless and Eggless Wholefood Vegetarian Meals with Plenty of Non-Dairy, Non-Wheaten Recipes

Helen Stephens

HYLAND HOUSE

First published in 1986 by
Hyland House Publishing Pty Limited
10 Hyland Street
South Yarra
Victoria 3141

National Library of Australia
cataloguing-in-publication data:

Stephens, Helen.
The Australian family vegetarian cookbook.

   Bibliography.
   Includes index.
   ISBN 0 908090 91 9.

1. Vegetarian cookery. 2. Cookery (Natural foods). I. Title.

641.5'636

Illustrated by Wendy Tapper
Cover design by Leonie Stott
Typeset by Kasia Graphics, Richmond, Melbourne
Printed by Koon Wah Printing Pty. Ltd., Singapore

Contents

To my three guinea pigs —
my two beautiful daughters, Emma and Mia;
and my wonderful, ever-patient husband,
Douglas, who luckily will eat anything
and everything.

Preamble

Anne and Al, the publishers, want me to tell you how I came to write this cookbook. I was undertaking a clearing-out fast — both physically and spiritually — and each day I meditated on things that I wanted to be rid of in my life. Well, it happened one day that, while trying to meditate as before, I could not bring my mind to bear on the things that I should have had in mind. Instead, each time I cleared my head to start afresh, a recipe popped into it. In the end I said, 'Okay God. I get the message. I'm supposed to stop this fast now and write a cookbook.'

It's now about two years on, and I have written the book, but I must also tell you that the rest of the recipes came into my head in just the same way as those original ones did, although not while actually meditating. I would simply stand in the kitchen and look around at the jars and things and the ideas would come. I guess most people would call that inspiration — but what is inspiration really? Whenever I made a boo-boo was it because of my intellect blocking out the messages?

Anne and Al also want me to tell you what sort of diet we follow in our family as it forms the basis for this book. I don't know whether you know *The Essene Gospel of Peace*; it was translated from Aramaic texts which were rediscovered this century after being lost for hundreds of years. They are the words of Jesus (Himself an Essene), and Book 1 sets out a health regime. It is very stringent indeed, stipulating how much to eat and how often, when to fast, limiting each meal to two or three different foods, banning foods out of season or from far away (like the macrobiotic and anthroposophic diets do), and setting out the manner in which one should eat (slowly and with reverence). While much of the regime does not suit our lifestyle, the part which we decided was imperative to follow was the injunction not to kill. In Jesus's words:

'God commanded your forefathers: "Thou shalt not kill." But their heart was hardened and they killed. Then Moses desired that at least they should not kill men, and he suffered them to kill beasts.... But I do say to you: Kill neither men, nor beasts, nor yet the food which goes into your mouth. For if you eat living food the same will quicken you, but if you kill your food, the dead food will kill you also. . . . For everything which kills your foods, kills your bodies also. And everything which kills your bodies kills your souls also. And your bodies become what your foods are, even as your spirits, likewise, become what your thoughts are. Therefore, eat not anything which fire, or frost, or water has destroyed. For burned, frozen and rotted foods will burn, freeze and rot your body also.'

Of all the passages which refer to no killing, I have purposely quoted this one as it goes on to say that you shouldn't cook or preserve foods, and we should certainly strive towards this ideal. In any case, whatever you decide is the right diet for your family, it is important to believe in it and to be positive about it, so that the right vibrations are in your food preparation. That's not to say that you shouldn't change your mind from time to time as new factors arise, but then you should throw yourself just as wholeheartedly into the changed diet.

To sum up the Essene diet, again in Jesus's words:

'So eat always from the table of God: the fruits of the trees, the grain and grasses of the field, the milk of the beasts, and the honey of bees.'

I recommend you buy *The Essene Gospel of Peace, Book 1,* which is available for under $2 at any new age bookshop. Also, turn up Genesis 1:29 to see what is laid down for diet there.

I must say, though, that we supplement our diet with minerals and a few vitamins, just because modern methods of agriculture deplete the soil so greatly. Figures from the US Department of Agriculture speak for themselves. An analysis for levels of essential minerals was carried out on 1 000 crop samples from farms in eleven midwestern states in the USA. In the following three years the process was repeated. This table shows the *decline* in food mineral levels which was found over the four years:

Sodium	55%	Iron	26%	Phosphorus	8%
Potassium	28%	Copper	68%	Magnesium	22%
Calcium	41%	Zinc	10%	Manganese	34%

The US Department of Agriculture states (in a report entitled *Human Nutrition, An Evaluation of Research in the United States* in Ashmead: *Chelated Mineral Nutrition:* p.5; *Institute* (1981)) that 'Most of the health problems underlying the leading causes of death in the United States could be modified by improvements in the diet.' and 'The highest death rate areas generally correspond to those where agriculturalists have recognised the soil as being depleted for several years.'

I won't go into the problem of why our agricultural methods are so bad, as many others have done so, but, if you're not convinced that we can no longer apply the maxim 'What was good enough for my grandparents is good enough for me,' then read M. Fukuoka's *One Straw Revolution.*

Introduction

There are three things wrong, to my mind, with many vegetarian cookbooks: first, not all the recipes are healthy; second, lots of kids hate the food (many has been the time when my own kids, Emma and Mia, rejected my cooking after all the labour that had gone into it), which brings me to the third point: *Lots of recipes are very labour intensive!* So, you chop and grind and mash and mix for so long that all the pleasure has gone out of it, and probably all the goodness, and you begin to wish for bygone days of meat and three veg.! In fact, it was just this huge amount of effort required to put together the dinner that made our family give up vegetarianism at one point in our lives when we had a baby and a toddler — two in nappies at the same time — and were renovating an old house on top of it all. When you've spent ages preparing the meal, hopping over tools in the kitchen, keeping the toddler out of holes in the floor, almost giving in and letting her play with the power points just to save her from braining the baby with a hammer, the last thing you want is to see the 'non-meat loaf' being rolled around a little mouth with distaste! It looked bad enough before, but wow, you should see it now. It's almost enough to send you gaga, but no, you simply revert to meat eating to save the day.

Well, no need to do that any more. Eating should be really simple. If it weren't for that nasty caveman who discovered fire, we would all be eating fruits and vegetables and nuts when we felt hungry. They really taste beautiful, but our palates have been ruined over the years and we expect cooked food. Indeed, many of us would be insulted if our friends served up a meal to us which took little or no preparation time. What a pity we can't learn to enjoy the food and be pleased that our friend has not had much work to do. Certainly we can all find out how to serve more simple and more nourishing foods to our own families. After all, *kids love simple, identifiable food.* Just pause to consider for a moment — do your children prefer a meal of casserole or a single food meal? Do they prefer lentil burgers or bread and cheese? Do they prefer cooked vegetables or raw ones? Well then, *take the hint;* serve simple, raw foods and you will all be happier and healthier.

It is interesting to read Dr Rita Leroi's outline of the dietary practice at the Lukas Klinik for Cancer Patients in her book, *An Anthroposophical Approach to Cancer:*

'We give special attention to a well balanced diet. Cancer patients are usually too much bound to earthly heaviness. For this reason, we try to avoid meat in our diet, this being a food which draws man down to earth and alienates him from his spiritual origins. We give cereals in a wide choice which, ripened by the sun, are rich in strengthening proteins and carbohydrates. We add salads and fresh vegetables from bio-dynamic farms. Roots activate the brain and thinking capacity, flowers stimulate the metabolism, and leaves are especially effective for the rhythmic system. Products of sour milk, yoghurt and different types of light cheese, and bread from rolled grain complete our meals. Instead of fat, we give olive and sunflower oils and some butter. We avoid artificially hardened fats, like margarine. For seasoning, we use herbs in great variety. Fruit juices provide for freshness. Tomatoes do not figure in our vegetable list — being proliferating nightshade plants and carcinogenic. Mushrooms, thriving in mouldy soil, are not on our diet. Mainly, we forbid alcohol in every form as weakening for forces of the ego.'

Shouldn't we practise food combining? Yes, if we are eating great mixtures of food, especially cooked food. However, if you sup on wholemeal bread, cheese and one or two raw fruits, and that is all, I guarantee that your stomach can cope with the mixture of high protein and high carbohydrate foods. On the other hand, if you are tempted to eat lasagne, followed by roast, followed by cheesecake and birthday cake, all swilled down with a glass or two of wine, and a cup of coffee to pick you up again — yes, your stomach will certainly have trouble and it would have been better to have planned your meal more carefully beforehand.

By now no doubt you'll be wondering why I bothered to write a cookbook at all when all I seem to be advocating is going to an apple tree and picking your own breakfast. The perfect situation would be just that (refer to *The Essene Gospel of Peace,* Book 1 and my preamble). However, as I said earlier, our tastes have been modified over the years and we expect cooked mixtures. Nevertheless, you will find that most of my recipes are simpler in content than others — certainly simpler to make — and once you have your family accustomed to eating more simply, keep the recipes for cooked concoctions for occasions when you *have* to cook.

Our family meals consist largely of a starch staple — cooked this way or that — with salad; very simple to be sure (and also very healthy). However, it has taken a lot of training in salad making and salad eating for the kids to be happy about having salads every day of their lives — even in Melbourne winters. It can be done by making salads interesting and by introducing them to the children gradually.

Because it is the main course which interests would-be vegetarian cooks, I have arranged this book so that they come first. As salads are so important, they come second. Third and fourth come 'Sauces and Dressings' and 'Finger Food Meals' as they can also contribute to the main course, as can 'Soups' and 'Breads and Pastries' which follow. The remaining sections are arranged in the way you'd expect: 'Desserts', 'Cakes, Cookies and Party Treats', 'Quick and Easy Bottles and Preserves' and finally 'Breakfasts'.

If you are currently running a meat and three veg. household and wish to change to healthy vegetarian food, please *first* make the change to wholemeal flour, pasta, brown rice, etc. It is harder to get used to the heavier, rougher taste and texture of these ingredients than it is to give up eating meat and it can take some months of gradual change before taste buds are no longer offended by the nutty flavours, and some months more before those same flavours are found superior and white bread starts to taste like a washing-up sponge. The same goes for replacing sugar with honey. Its more definite flavour seems too strong for some people. Of course, it is impossible to make some foods like sponge cake with honey! But that's just tough; it's far better to have a whole food than a refined one; see the chapter on desserts. Believe it or not, there'll come a time when exquisite, sophisticated French cuisine will taste empty or dead and you will be hankering after some live food with real vibrations — something to get your choppers really stuck into! And here's something to get your brain really stuck into:

'. . . we must . . . see that every inadequate food quality, every inappropriate process to which food has been subjected before it gets to us, every remnant of poisonous substances, everything that removes food from its archetypal image, makes it into a distorted image; thus progressively weakening the individual mechanism of the body in the breakdown of food and the build up of nutriment for the process of the Body, Soul and Ego organisation.' This germane statement is from an article by Margaret Curl on nutrition in *The Melbourne Therapy Centre for Cancer and Other Patients Newsletter,* Vol. 4, No. 2.

And finally a note about expense. Some people have asked how we can afford to eat all those expensive ingredients, but let me assure you, wonderful, living nuts and vegetables and fruits are not nearly so expensive as dead animal flesh. If you are really hard up, you can still live like a king with only the occasional splurge on nuts (instead of chocolates in front of the telly perhaps). Find a food co-operative to have the enjoyment of working with people with similar ideals and save money because of its bulk purchasing power. Go to a market for your fruit and vegetables. Some say it's not worth the petrol money, but you've only got to save $2 on half a kilo of snow peas and you've saved your petrol money.

I wish you all love and luck in building the bodies of the next generation into a humane humanity.

Protein

But, what about protein? I hear you say. I would refer everyone to Chapter 2 of Paavo Airola's book, *Are You Confused*, for clarification of this issue, and many others.

I might just add here that, at one time in our family, we began complementing amino acids in proteins — adding milk powder to this, or seeds to that — to ensure that we had enough protein, because we had read about how vegetable protein was insufficient to sustain life, etc. The outcome was that we became a bit neurotic with all the counting of grams of usable protein and, in addition, I put on eight kilos for my efforts! Needless to say, we soon abandoned that attempt — but unfortunately, once again, we gave in and became meat eaters, something we did not want to do but, at the time, we were hoodwinked into thinking that we needed to worry about the kids getting enough protein.

Since last century everyone seems to have been brainwashed from schooldays into believing that animal protein is the only complete protein, whereas recent research (quoted in Paavo Airola's *Hypoglycemia: A Better Approach*) shows that: 'Vegetable foods which contain all eight essential amino acids, and, therefore, are complete protein foods, are soybeans, peanuts, almonds, buckwheat, sunflower seeds, pumpkin seeds, potatoes, avocadoes, and all green leafy vegetables.' Airola further says in *Are You Confused?* that: 'You need only one-half the amount of protein if you eat raw vegetable proteins instead of cooked animal proteins,' and 'It is virtually impossible not to get enough protein in your diet provided you have enough to eat of natural, unrefined foods.'

So now our family relies on Mother Nature. She put protein into every cell of all the fruit and vegetables and She made the colours attractive so that we might be induced to eat Her produce in its natural state. As long as we go along with Her as often as possible, we can't go wrong. (See *The Essene Gospel of Peace*, Book 1 and my preamble.)

Butter versus Margarine

Butter is better. Even though I have a milk allergy, I wouldn't consider substituting artificial margarine with all its chemical nasties. Maureen Minchin has described how a certain level of allergens may be ingested before any ill effects are noticed. Butter must be top on the priority list of foods you are going to allow yourself.

If for no other reason, you should use butter because of the packaging. Margarine plastic containers pollute the environment. Butter papers can be stored in the door of the refrigerator until they are needed for lining a cake tin. They also help light an obstinate fire.

Sugar

I will have to watch what I write here as I am so steamed up about sugar that I could go on for pages!

First, let me tell you that sugar and honey are *not* as bad as each other as most people in the community believe. It is true that they are both absorbed too readily by the body and they are therefore damaging to the pancreas and the liver. It is true also that they are both damaging to teeth — in fact, honey on bread or, worse, on dummies, is probably more damaging because of its sticky nature. Of course, honey used as a sweetener in cakes, for instance, is no stickier on the teeth than sugar.

However, *here's the big difference!* Honey is a pure food but sugar has been so refined that it wreaks havoc in the body.

It is commonly believed that sugar is no more than 'empty calories', but in fact it is a lethal substance. According to William Dufty in *Sugar Blues*, sugar leeches out the B group vitamins during ingestion and 'Minerals such as sodium, potassium and magnesium, and calcium are mobilized and used in chemical transmutation.'

You would not knowingly give your children other chemicals which have been proved to do all these things, would you? And when you learn about sugar's effects, you won't be using it again I expect. For proof, or just light fascinating reading, I recommend that you read *Sugar Blues*. Also, if you have a real sweet tooth and want more sugar-free recipes than I give, try Janet Horsley's *Sugar-Free Cookbook* which gives lots of yummy recipes.

There are children of my acquaintance whose behaviour has been improved when taken off all sugar and allowed just a little honey each day instead. I myself am hypoglycaemic and therefore any simple sugar is a problem for my body. And, if I ever do ingest sugar, I can barely control my temper. I hate myself at the time, but just have to pick on everyone and even yell and scream. On the other hand, if I have a splurge on honey, my body copes well. No doubt, if I were to continue to splurge, after a couple of days I would experience problems. Another interesting thing is that the only time I ever crave a cigarette (having given up smoking over two years ago) is the day after I have eaten sugar. It took me a long while to wake up to this. I couldn't work out why, seemingly for no reason, I suddenly wanted to smoke again, and then I realised that it was always the day after I had been visiting and had had a slice of someone else's cake! (Interestingly, William Dufty points out that cigarette tobacco is sugar cured, and, furthermore, in countries where the tobacco is not so treated, there is no correlation between smoking and lung cancer.)

Most drug users, alcoholics and habitual criminals would not be where they are today if it were not for sugar. Sugar should be banned as a food and developed into an alternative to petrol for fuelling our cars!

Food Allergies

Unfortunately, today's children are prone to food allergies, with milk products, wheat, yeast, acid fruits and sugar being the biggest offenders. It has taken many mothers a long long time to wake up to the fact that their children are allergic to something in their diet, largely, I suppose, because we weren't afflicted with allergies much in our generation. However, it has been found that, as well as a runny nose and constant cold, the ingestion of allergens (foods to which we are allergic) can be the cause of poor school performance, irritability, hyperactivity, extremely anti-social behaviour, tummy ache, insomnia, drowsiness, sluggishness, and so the list goes on. Actually, many mothers are now finding that their general lack of stamina is also because they themselves have developed allergic reactions to food or the environment. So, if you're finding it hard to cope with the kids, you are probably *not* inadequate as you've been thinking; you may just have allergies.

One can only conjecture about the cause of all these allergies. It has to be something pretty widespread, if not universal, to affect so many people. In addition, it has to be something which was not prevalent when we were growing up.

Maureen Minchin in her excellent book, *Food for Thought*, suggests that it is because many of today's mothers were bottle-fed when they themselves were infants. I believe, though, that there are other concomitant causes, as I know Mrs Minchin does too.

Recent research by Steven Rochlitz has shown that the toxic effects of chemical substances called *aldehydes* — released from synthetics and from the micro-organism *Candida albicans* — interfere with correct integration of the two hemispheres of the brain and therefore weaken the body's innate ability to mobilise its immune system against allergens.

William Dufty in *Sugar Blues* suggests that allergies are part and parcel of what we can expect when our systems 'jack up' from sugar abuse. Maybe he's right and sugar is the bottom line. After all, bottle infant formulae are packed with sugar. Also it appears that the overgrowth of *Candida albicans* present in the gut of allergy-afflicted people feeds on sugar, among other things.

Whatever the cause or causes, there are many things that can be done to help. In the meantime, I hope that some of the recipes in this book may be helpful, as none includes eggs or sugar and many offer alternatives to wheat and dairy products. Those recipes which are non-wheaten and non-dairy are marked with symbols in the contents pages. Although butter is obviously a dairy product, where it is the only dairy product in a recipe, I have marked it as non-dairy because it is so easily substituted for — but, before replacing it, please read my comments on butter, page 6.

The whole allergy problem is so new and so much is continuously being discovered that it is hard to know what to write about and what to leave out, but I think it worthwhile to mention that, in our own family experience, we have found that when our water purifier is out of action for a couple of days our symptoms are suddenly much worse, even though we seem to be ingesting the usual modicum of allergens. I would therefore advise anyone plagued with allergy problems to invest in an ion exchange water purifier which removes the chemicals in the water, and to use this for all cooking and drinking water. If you are then worried about your children getting insufficient fluoride, you can buy calcium fluoride tablets from your health food store. Calcium fluoride is available in a natural, colloidal form just as the body uses it. Any excess is eliminated easily by your body and not stored in the joints like the fluoride in the water supply. (People with bad arthritis, for instance, have found that their condition becomes much worse when they drink fluoridated water.)

Finally, let me say that I have fairly recently experienced definite relief from allergy reactions by using *Touch for Health* which is a self-help system of healing. After attending a twelve-hour class you have the basic skills to help yourself on the road to health. If you attend with a partner, that's even better, as the benefit for each of you is more than doubled. *Touch for Health* puts healing where it should be — with the people. It is described in the *Touch for Health Association, Victoria, Newsletter* as 'a practical guide to natural preventative health care.... (It) uses a series of muscle tests to obtain direct feedback from the body .... we can detect physical, emotional or chemical imbalance. When weakness or imbalance is found we activate certain points on the body with deep massage or light touch to correct it and restore the body's natural energy flow.'

Cooking Notes

EQUIPMENT

Blenders or Food Processors: Food processors seem to have largely replaced blenders these days, but there is one job which the blender does and the food processor does not — grinding seeds to a paste as required in making mustard. Generally, they both work with a metal blade whizzing around the bottom of the bowl or goblet which chops and grinds and mashes. However, the blender does this more effectively and therefore has to be watched closely when in action for fear the solids end up liquefied. In addition, a food processor has a range of different blades which can be used to produce different results like grating and slicing.

The only things which can be done by a conventional beater and cannot be handled by the food processor are whipping cream and stiffening egg whites. Otherwise, all beating jobs can be accomplished. So, in effect, a food processor is a blender and a beater in one.

Many people will not use food processors or blenders, or, for that matter, any electric device, because they prefer to impart their own loving vibrations to the food being prepared and because the vibrations of electric motors are coarse and harsh. In principle this is true. However, most people who advocate this chopping and slicing by hand are forced, because of lack of time or other constraints, to make sacrifices in other areas. For instance, many people do not make their own bread or yoghurt or sauce or tofu. They do not stop to think that there must be many coarse, and maybe even negative vibrations put into their bought goods. I maintain that a food processor speeds things up so greatly that the cook has more time to devote to other basic needs or, if she is not inclined to do more cooking, she might be better off meditating for some part of the day so that she gets her own vibrations into good working order. Therefore, I have designed many recipes for use with a food processor or blender.

Cooking Pots: Have you a favourite earthenware casserole dish which seems to cook any recipe better than other dishes? Rudolf Hauschka's experiments show that earthenware is second only to, would you believe it, gold as a food vessel, followed by porcelain, enamel, glass, copper, tin, iron and aluminium. I was not at all surprised to see that aluminium comes last. It feels nasty and is hard to clean and marks easily. Although iron is only second-last, stainless steel saucepans are far superior to aluminium and it is much easier to be a good cook with better saucepans. White sauces, for instance, seem to stick and lump more easily in aluminium. So please invest in some better pots if yours are aluminium. Perhaps gold is a bit out of your reach, but stainless steel or glass for the cooking top and earthenware for the oven should be attainable for just about everyone.

INGREDIENTS

Anne from Hyland House, in her thoroughness, asked me to include some notes on the ingredients. In this day and age I doubt whether you'll have any trouble finding any of the ingredients, but I'll tell you about a few things anyway. I must say, though, that just about everything I use in my recipes can be found at the health food shop. If you cannot locate something elsewhere, or have never heard of it, ask your local health food shop. You get friendly old fashioned service from them. One or two items are available only from Asian groceries, i.e., Asian tofu and the items mentioned in Stir Fries (recipe 17).

Agar (or, more correctly, agar agar) dissolves in boiling water and sets when it is lukewarm. It is a seaweed derivative, is available unbleached from health food stores and, of course, is the vegetarian substitute for the animal-hoof gelatine. On top of that, I find it easier to use than gelatine. The amounts needed vary a little from brand to brand, but, as a guide, a teaspoon of powdered agar gels one cup of liquid, whereas it takes one tablespoon of flakes to do the same job.

Black Pepper is a bit burny for the tummy and therefore should be used sparingly. Whenever possible substitute red pepper or a mixture of black pepper and whole allspice (pimento). If you will bear with me, I'll tell you how I came to use a mixture in our pepper mill. When Emma was a toddler she got into my herbs and spices and tipped out the black pepper and the whole allspice which, as you know, look quite similar. As I had largish containers of each, didn't want to waste them and couldn't be bothered sorting them out, they all went into the pepper container where they were used as pepper. That was over ten years ago and I am still using the same mixture. I found that they are really nice together and the allspice 'waters down' the pepper so that its effect is not so harmful. You will gather, though, that we don't use very much black pepper in our house.

Flour: We are lucky to have available to us in Australia good organically grown flour which has been stone ground. Therefore, there is no excuse, to my mind, for accepting any old wholemeal flour. Why not go even one better than organically grown and use biodynamic flour?

Fruit juice concentrates: These can be bought at the health food shop and are very handy for camping and for storing for an emergency. There is a trend these days to use them for sweetening in recipes and, indeed, I have done so on a couple of occasions myself. However, I still prefer to go for the really natural ingredients like honey and maple syrup as, while fruit juice concentrates are obviously from natural ingredients, they have been tampered with by man. Meddling man has mucked up enough of this planet — don't let's encourage him any more than we have to.

Margarine: See Butter versus Margarine, page 6.

Miso is a paste made of fermented soy beans, plus grains and sea salt. It is very salty. There are several different strengths. The darker it is, the saltier it is, and the darker miso is usually used in cold weather while white miso is used in summer. It is available from health food shops and Asian groceries. Don't be frightened to buy some because you will find it very useful for knocking up a quick hearty soup — just add vegetables and hot water. Keep it in the refrigerator door so that you always have it on hand — you'll be surprised at the uses you find for it.

Soy Sauce: Everyone is aware of the soy sauce in little bottles on tables at Chinese restaurants, but read the labels before buying your next bottle. Go for one that is naturally fermented and, if possible, salt reduced. Tamari is the name given to many naturally fermented soy sauces, but others are available. Soy sauce of any sort is made by fermenting soya beans and grains and adding sea salt and water.

Tofu, which is soy bean curd, is curdled with nigari (the leftover product of sea salt refining) or calcium sulphate (gypsum). The former is available from health food shops and is much firmer and less bland than the latter, available at Asian groceries (or, if you live in the country and have no close Asian groceries, try the local Chinese restaurant).

The nigari tofu is excellent for frying and grilling, being firmer and easier to handle. If you do intend frying it, fry the large surfaces of the whole block first before cutting it up — there is nothing more tedious than trying to fry all six sides of sixty-four cubes!

Asian tofu is soft and floppy and hard to fry, but it is an absolute must for the sauces and dressings in this book as it blends to a very smooth texture and is tasteless.

If you cannot locate Asian tofu then you can use the following substitute, but I warn you that it is not as good, being a lot less bland. You therefore must not try to use it with a very subtly flavoured dish such as Mandarin Orange Sauce (recipe 61):

Mix 2 tablespoons soy flour with a scant half cup of cold water in a small saucepan and put over a low heat, stirring until the mixture bubbles. Continue stirring and cooking for a further minute or two. Use when cool.

Zest: Very fine peelings of lemon and orange rind.

METHOD

When Hyland House asked me to include a few notes on how to paper a cake tin, etc., I thought they were going too far, until I remembered that I couldn't cook when I was first married. We lived in the country and I was forever phoning my mother long distance to find out how to do something or other, as books didn't always help. If only I could remember now just what it is that new cooks need to know, but I will make do with how to paper a cake tin, make pastry and make a white sauce using the roux method.

How to Paper a Cake Tin

When I was little, I used to watch my grandmother papering large round tins for fruit cakes. She used brown paper and carefully cut a circle a centimetre or so larger than the base of the tin and then cut little nicks in that extra width so that it would fold up the sides of the tin and sit flat. She then cut a long strip that would fit exactly around the sides. It was all quite an operation, but time seemed more plentiful in those days, even despite the unavailability of modern labour-saving devices. These days, the availability of spring form pans (cake tins with removable bases) helps things along. If you give your pan a quick butter over all and then sit a bit of butter paper in the bottom (print side out) that should do the trick for round tins.

Loaf tins are a little trickier if you want to ensure that your cake or loaf comes out without any mishaps. I find the quickest way is to take a piece of butter paper and fold it into a 'U' shape so that it starts down one side of the tin, goes across the bottom and up the other side. You will have to trim it a little on the side if its width is too great for the length of the cake tin. If you want a really foolproof job, repeat the process lengthwise for the loaf tin, but a good smear of butter will probably do. Really, all the paper may do is give you a 'handle' to help to get the cake out.

Remove the paper before the cake becomes completely cold, as with many recipes it sticks when cold, and, believe me, the paper tends to mar the effect of the delicious cake — it's a bit on the chewy side.

How to Make Pastry

Pastry, a flour and water dough with a raising agent and shortening (fat) as a lightening ingredient, is touchy to make. If you get it too hot or overwork it, it becomes tough, because you will have melted the little lumps of butter and started bringing out the gluten in the grain, something which is most desirable for breadmaking but not for pastry. Some people use ice cubes in a hollow pastry roller (or corked bottle) and even roll their pastry on a cold marble slab with hands previously dipped in cold water. I think you can achieve a satisfactory result without all that, but just don't knead it or work it for too long or on a scorcher of a day.

The butter should be cut in even-sized pieces and then thrown in with the well mixed or sieved dry ingredients. Then the butter is rubbed between your cool fingers until it is broken up into smallish lumps — about split pea size I suppose. Alternatively, this can be done with two knives to cut the butter in, especially if your hands are hot, or in the food processor by turning the motor on and off rapidly, 'pulsing' it, as the manufacturers put it in the instruction books.

Then the water is mixed in — once again without dilly-dallying — and the soft dough which results is rolled out on a floured board with a floured rolling pin. Remember to flour your hands. Alternatively, the dough can be rolled between two sheets of plastic or waxed lunch wrap — a necessity sometimes with wholemeal flour, as it is more difficult to handle.

Pastry should not be cooked at too low a temperature or else this too will toughen it, but I find that the very hot oven (200°C) recommended in old books tends to overcook the filling; so I recommend 190°C/375°F as a happy medium.

There is no need to grease the pie plate when the pastry is rich enough with shortening (fat), and these days nobody scrimps on butter, as was done in war years, for instance. So I don't think you'll find any modern pastry recipes that would stick to the pan.

How to Make a White Sauce Using the Roux Method

A roux is a thickening made with flour and fat. The fat is melted and the flour is stirred in and cooked, stirring almost constantly, for a couple of minutes so that no 'raw' flavour comes through the finished sauce. Liquid, commonly milk, is then added — all at once if quite cold, or in stages if not — and the sauce is then stirred almost constantly again while being heated. Once the sauce commences to bubble or 'blomp', it is as thick as it will get (remember all sauces are thicker when cold, but they are usually used hot). So if it is too thick, add more liquid and stir until the blomping starts again.

Hints on how to get kids to eat unloved foods

I believe that we as 'nurturers' are responsible for our family's health and hence what they eat. It is not good enough to let them snack on whatever they fancy and skip the vegies at dinner time. We can all have our palates spoiled too easily and many kids will opt for cookies, Vegemite sandwiches and lemonade. Perhaps they don't even have the imagination to think of alternatives.

On the other hand, I don't advocate standover tactics, although I must confess to having used them on the odd occasion, but have found a little native cunning, or even downright trickery, doesn't go astray. That's where the following hints will come in handy. Also, consult the page headed 'What *do* kids like to eat!'

I would like to quote from *Nutrition* by Rudolf Hauschka (actually, this part comes from the addendum to the book written by Grethe Hauschka, M.D.):

'A sensible management of youthful diets can prevent much later illness, while indifference lays the basis for it. It is most important here to make wise and patient efforts to overcome the food dislikes so often found in children, lest they become fixed in harmful one-sidedness. Tiny tastes of the food they think they cannot bear help the organism to adjust to and gradually get to like it. Tact, fantasy and fondness do wonders for the child, for every single food that a person becomes able to digest and like makes its special contribution to that individual's very real and important capacity to deal with and gain mastery over matter. This is far kinder than weakly giving in to children's whims. There is room for just as much courageous and adventurous action on the child's part here as his heroes ever demonstrated in meeting their challenges.'

Here are my hints:
1. Smother the food with a well-loved sauce. Gradually decrease the amount of sauce as the food is tolerated.

2. Hide it — in a pie,
> — in a savoury pancake (see Idea Z, Twenty-six More Ideas)
> — in a pastry roll (see Idea Y, Twenty-six More Ideas)

3. Serve the unloved food with a favourite food on condition that the 'goodies' have to be eaten with the 'baddies'. For example, Mia adores spring onion and hates avocado. When the rest of the family eats avocado I like Mia to have a little also as the meal is planned around the avocado. Therefore she gets a spring onion to eat with her slice so that the strong onion flavour well and truly hides the subtle avocado flavour.

   Pizza is a good vehicle for putting lots of 'goodies' with one 'baddy'.

4. Another trick I used to play on Mia was to make an avocado dressing with usually just pureed avocado, oil and lemon juice and parsley as ingredients. I made sure she saw me putting in the parsley and told her it was a parsley dressing. She therefore ate and enjoyed it with the rest of the family, believing the green colour to be dye from the parsley.

   A cunning trick with zucchini is to slice off the tell-tale green skin.

5. Many of us dislike the unknown. Take the kids to a Middle Eastern restaurant for dinner a few times and they will get to like the flavours served there and then like them at home also.

6. Camouflage the problem food by serving it with some stronger flavours as in Mystery Vegetable Soup (recipe 80) and Potato Soup (recipe 82).

7. Trade off — serve one 'goody' with a whole host of 'baddies', see my idea for an Indian feast under Dhall (recipe 21).

What _do_ kids like to eat?

Most children, despite their various food fads, eat and enjoy the foods in the table below. Alongside each food are numbers referring to the recipes which feature that particular food (the letters refer to the Twenty-six More Ideas for Main Meals). Therefore, if your child is a problem eater but loves certain items, look over this table to locate the recipes he/she is likely to enjoy. I have not included sweets for obvious reasons.

Bread, crackers, etc.
11, 18, 49
B, I, T, Y, Z
Cheese
1, 2, 3, 4, 6, 9, 10, 18, 22, 23,
24, 25, 33, 36, 37, 46, 48, 50,
56, 60, 79, 80
B, D, G, I, U, W, Y, Z
Fried foods
19, 20, 51
K
Noodles
17, 22, 23, 46, 47, 79, 80
J
Nuts
7, 27, 37, 38, 52, 71
H, M, N, O

Pickles, gherkins, etc.
17, 40, 73, 76, 77
Potato
1, 8, 9, 11, 12, 16, 26, 29, 31,
32, 51, 74, 79, 82
E, Q, X
Rice
2, 4, 5, 7, 15, 16, 17, 33, 37,
41, 48
A, C, H, L
Tomato
6, 9, 10, 11, 18, 22, 24, 26, 36,
38, 39, 41, 42, 47, 50, 54, 59,
68, 72, 79, 80
B, D, G, M, Q, S, W

How to use up leftovers, unwanted vegetable pieces, stale bread and over-ripe fruit

The numbers refer to the recipes, the letters to the Twenty-six More Ideas for Main Meals.

Cooked beans
(less than 2 cups)
54,
A, D, G, H
Cooked beetroot
76,
O
Cooked brown lentils
(less than 2 cups)
S
Cooked potatoes
(less than 2 cups)
16, 74, 76
Cooked red lentils
(less than 2 cups
73
Cooked rice (or other grains)
(less than 2 cups)
A, C, H, L, W
Excess pastry
B, P, Q

Leftover vanilla custard
109
Outside lettuce leaves
1, 17, 80, 83
K, U, Z
Over-ripe bananas
96, 98, 103, 104, 105, 110,
117, 118, 147
Over-ripe pears
75, 96, 147
Silverbeet stalks
3, 17, 80, 83, 141, 142
K, Z
Stale or flopped bread
11
B
Unwanted vegetable pieces
17, 20, 80, 83, 141, 142
B, K, U, Z

Main Meals and Vegetable Dishes

LETTUCE PIE

1.

Serves 4

If you grow your own lettuces, you will have many outside leaves which usually either go to waste or to the compost or the chooks — but it is the outside leaves which contain the most goodness! Even when you buy your vegetables, you should buy lettuces with their outside leaves intact. That way you can tell whether your lettuce is fresh or not, as these leaves wilt well before the inner ones, and the wily retailer strips them off.

Filling:
350 g outside lettuce leaves
600 g potato — sliced
2 tablespoons oil
1 clove garlic — finely chopped
250 g zucchini — finely sliced
50 g shelled peas
2 teaspoons kelp granules
250 g ricotta cheese

Topping:
1 cup grated cheese (about 100 g)
40 g butter
2 cups rolled oats

After washing the lettuce leaves well, place them in a saucepan with a little water and a close fitting lid. Bring the water to steaming point and then remove the leaves and put them to one side. In the same saucepan and with the same liquid cook the potatoes. Add more liquid if required. Meanwhile, heat the oil in a large pan and saute the finely chopped clove of garlic and the finely sliced zucchini for 5 or 10 minutes — until the zucchini is a little soft. Then add the peas and kelp and mix well.

When the potatoes are soft, mash them with the ricotta and then roughly chop the limp lettuce leaves and add them to the mashed potato mixture which should then be combined with the zucchini and pea mixture. Mix well.

Oil a deep pie dish, say 20 x 25 cm, and spread the mixture in.

Now mix all the topping ingredients together well. The topping is then spread over the pie which is put in a moderate oven (180°C/350°F) for about 25-30 minutes until heated through and the top is starting to brown.

2. SPINACH PIE

Serves 4-6

Don't worry if your children don't like spinach, as the spinach is almost unrecognisable in this recipe.

250 g spinach leaf
1 tablespoon butter
100 g Australian gouda   cheese
— grated
¼ teaspoon grated nutmeg

2 to 3 cups cooked brown rice
(or mixed steamed grains such
as barley, rye, buckwheat)
Wholemeal Pastry (recipe 84)
(or Non-Wheaten Pastry
(recipe 85))

This pie can be completely encased in wholemeal pastry or, for a less filling meal, simply cover the top of the dish with pastry. Alternatively, the base of the pie can be pastry and cheese can be melted on top. Whatever you do, a 20 cm (approximately) pie plate is needed.

Wash, chop and drain the spinach and then saute in the butter in a wide-based saucepan. Stir in the grated cheese and nutmeg. Finally, mix the rice or other grains in well, place in the pie plate and cover with pastry.

Bake in a moderate oven (180°C/350°F) for 30-40 minutes until the pastry is cooked.

3. ZUCCHINI PIE

Serves 4

This recipe fairly camouflages the zucchini.

Filling:
2 tablespoons butter
75 g semolina (or brown rice
flour may be substituted)
200 ml water or milk or a
mixture of both
1 tablespoon Honey Mustard
(recipe 139)
1 dessertspoon Herbed Apple
Cider Vinegar (recipe 146)
250 g zucchini — thinly sliced
150 g silver beet stalks — thinly
sliced (or an extra 150 g
zucchini)

Topping:
1 cup rolled oats
½ cup wheatgerm (or millet
flakes may be substituted)
1 cup grated cheese
2 tablespoons melted butter

To make the filling, melt the butter, add the semolina and cook over a moderate heat for a couple of minutes. Now add the water/milk — all at once if cold or in stages if warm — and stir until the sauce thickens. Then add the mustard and vinegar and taste to see if seasonings need to be adjusted before proceeding.

Mix the vegetables with the sauce and pour into a 20 cm pie plate, which can have its bottom lined with pastry if you prefer.

Mix all the topping ingredients together and pat them into place on top of the pie.

Cook the pie in a moderate oven (180°C/350°F) for 30-40 minutes until the zucchini is soft and the top browned.

SIMPLE STAPLE

4.

Serves 4-6

The name speaks for itself, but it doesn't tell you how tasty it is. Just looking at the list of ingredients you'd be forgiven for thinking it looks dull, but try it — you'll be surprised.

Use any cooked grain. I prefer a mixture, usually hulled millet and brown rice. Serve with a crisp salad.

4 cups cooked grain
1 clove garlic — crushed
1 tablespoon chopped fresh
parsley

1 tablespoon dried basil
1 cup sesame seeds
200 g tasty cheese — grated

Oil a large baking dish and spread the cooked grain over it so that it is about 1 cm thick — definitely not more than 1.5 cm.

Combine all remaining ingredients and spread over the top of the grain.

Heat in a moderate oven (180°C/350°F) until the grain is warm and the cheese melted.

5. *QUICK CASSEROLE*

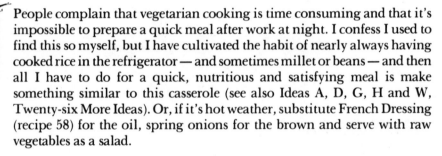

Serves 4

People complain that vegetarian cooking is time consuming and that it's impossible to prepare a quick meal after work at night. I confess I used to find this so myself, but I have cultivated the habit of nearly always having cooked rice in the refrigerator — and sometimes millet or beans — and then all I have to do for a quick, nutritious and satisfying meal is make something similar to this casserole (see also Ideas A, D, G, H and W, Twenty-six More Ideas). Or, if it's hot weather, substitute French Dressing (recipe 58) for the oil, spring onions for the brown and serve with raw vegetables as a salad.

3 tablespoons oil
1 teaspoon sweet red paprika
3 teaspoons ground cumin
1 brown onion — chopped
5 small zucchini
10 stoned black olives —
  chopped

3 very ripe tomatoes
2 stalks celery, including tops
1 cup bean shoots
¾ cup Brazil nuts — roughly
  chopped
2-3 cups cooked brown rice

Heat the oil in a large flameproof casserole, add spices and saute the chopped onion. Slice the zucchini and stir in with the onion until well coated with the oil and spices. Put the lid on and leave to simmer while chopping the olives. Stir these in, replace the lid and chop the tomatoes and celery. Now stir these in and replace the lid for a minute or two until they are warmed through.

Finally stir in the bean shoots, roughly chopped nuts and the rice, and serve when hot.

CHICKPEA BAKE
Serves 4-6

6.

Quite an economical family meal which is quick to whip up.

50 g butter
1 average leek — sliced
½ average red pepper —chopped
2 pinches dried oregano
1 teaspoon sweet red paprika
2 small to average zucchini
— sliced

4 cups roughly chopped celery
tops
3 large tomatoes — roughly
chopped
2 cups cooked drained
chickpeas (about ⅔ cup raw)
150 g cheese — grated
1½ cups wholemeal or rye
breadcrumbs

Melt the butter in a large saucepan and saute the leek and pepper with the oregano and paprika. While these are softening, add the zucchini and, when the zucchini is in turn softened, add the celery tops and stir them through. Finally stir in the tomatoes and chickpeas.

Turn the mixture into a large baking dish (preferably earthenware) and top with the grated cheese and breadcrumbs which have been mixed together.

Bake in a moderate oven (180°C/350°F) until the mixture is heated through and the cheese is melted.

NUTTY BROCCOLI
Serves 4

7.

1 clove garlic — crushed
¼ teaspoon ground cumin
½ cup butter and oil mixed (see
Butter versus Margarine)

½ cup walnut pieces
½ cup almonds
2 cups cooked brown rice
3-4 cups of flowerets and 2 cm
stem pieces of broccoli —
lightly steamed

Using a large saucepan or frying pan saute the garlic and cumin in the butter/oil mixture and then add the nuts. Next stir in the rice and, as soon as it is heated, stir the broccoli through. Serve when hot.

8. *SCALLOPED POTATOES*

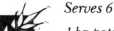

Serves 6

1 kg potatoes
1 good handful fresh herbs —
finely chopped
1 clove garlic — crushed

500 ml milk
vegetable salt to taste
butter for garnish

Wash potatoes and slice them finely. Now wash them again to remove most of the surplus starch. Allow them to dry off on the sink a bit. Meanwhile finely chop the herbs and crush the garlic and mix these with the milk.

Now place a layer of the potatoes in a well greased baking dish, sprinkle with a little vegetable salt and pour some of the milk mixture over. Lay down another layer of potatoes and repeat the process until all the ingredients are used up, and then dot the top with butter.

You may, if you prefer, put grated cheese on top, but then omit the vegetable salt between the layers.

Cook in a moderate oven (180°C/350°F) until soft but not sloppy.

Some potatoes will absorb more liquid than others and so the milk mixture may be too much sometimes. Use any left over for soup stock.

9. *ITALIAN POTATOES*

Serves 6

1 kg potatoes — scrubbed and
cut into ½ cm slices
1-2 tablespoons oil
1 bay leaf
3 tablespoons dehydrated
tomato flakes

8 stoned black olives — chopped
boiling water
½ to 1 cup wheat germ (or millet
flakes), depending on size of
dish used
cheese — grated

Using a large-based flameproof casserole or au gratin dish, saute potato slices in a couple of tablespoons of oil for 1 to 2 minutes each side. If they won't all fit in at once, do them in stages, removing the first batch to make room for the second, and so on. If necessary, add more oil for each batch.

Now, with all the potatoes in the dish, add the bay leaf, tomato flakes and chopped olives and enough boiling water to barely cover the mixture. Simmer for 15 minutes if your dish is lidded, or 20 minutes if not.

Pour off most of the liquid and reserve for soup stock. Add a generous layer of wheat germ on top and finish off with grated or thinly sliced cheese. Place in a moderate oven (180°C/350°F) for 10 to 15 minutes until the cheese is bubbly and has released some of its fat into the wheat germ — yum!

I usually like the salad to present a contrast to the main meal, but this is best I think with a tossed salad containing more olives and tomatoes.

MOCK TURKEY 10.
Yield: 2 cups

You may recall this recipe from days gone by. My mother used to make ribbon sandwiches with mock turkey (or mock chicken which is the same, I think). However, I have discovered that it is really much more versatile; not just a sandwich filling.

The filling can be put in celery sticks and on crackers as an appetiser. Or you can also use it hot, as an instant 'stuffing', spread on cooked zucchini which has been cut in half lengthwise, or you can make it a bit runnier (by adding liquid or more tomato) and use it as a sauce for hot broccoli, for instance.

I found out, too, that mock turkey can be turned into a 'meat' loaf. When it is cold it becomes quite firm and its texture and colour are a little akin to — horror of horrors — camp pie. I hasten to add that it tastes a thousand times better.

1 small onion — finely chopped	*1 teaspoon dried basil*
1 tablespoon oil	*1 cup grated cheese (about*
2 small tomatoes — finely	*100 g)*
chopped	*1 cup wholemeal breadcrumbs*
½ teaspoon dried marjoram	*or wheat germ or any soft*
	cooked grain

Using a medium large saucepan, saute the onion in the oil until soft and then add the tomatoes and herbs and simmer for a few minutes. Remove pan from heat and add cheese and crumbs/grain and stir in until a gooey, homogenous mess results.

If you want to turn it into a loaf, butter a small terrine and dust it with fine breadcrumbs and then put the mixture in this dish to cool in the refrigerator. When quite cold and firm, turn out onto a serving platter. Alternatively, you could 'sculpt' the mixture directly onto the serving platter.

11. ISLANDS

Serves 4-8

This is a quaint lunchtime dish which appeals to the kids.

*1½ times the recipe for
  Uncooked Tomato Sauce
  (recipe 59)
2-3 teaspoons sweet red paprika*

*8 thinnish slices of whole wheat
  (or rye) bread
Herbed Potato Dip (recipe 74)*

Season the Uncooked Tomato Sauce with the paprika and spread it out in a large baking dish (big enough to take the eight slices of bread).

Spread the bread with Herbed Potato Dip and float the resulting green islands in the red sea. Heat in a moderate oven (180°C/350°F) until warmed through.

12. POTATO PATTIES

Yield: 12 generous patties

*1 kg potatoes
2 onions
½ cup chopped fresh parsley
1 teaspoon dried mixed herbs
1 teaspoon sweet red paprika
1 teaspoon celery seed*

*1 tablespoon kelp granules
1 good cup wheat germ (or
  millet flakes)
1 cup soy flour
oil for frying*

Grate the raw potatoes and onions and mix well with the seasonings. Add the wheat germ or millet flakes and, after mixing that in thoroughly, mix in the soy flour.

Form into patties and fry in a heavy pan over a low to moderate heat until the potatoes are cooked. Serve with vegetable salt.

PUMPKIN PATTIES
Yield: 16 patties

(13.)

These are tasty; they also camouflage the flavour of the pumpkin so that pumpkin haters will eat them.

2 cups cooked, mashed	*1 teaspoon sea salt*
pumpkin (about 500 g)	*1 cup rolled oats*
1 medium brown onion	*½ cup soy flour*
— minced	*½ cup gluten flour*
1 clove garlic — crushed	*½ cup wholemeal plain flour*
1 long stick celery — minced	*oil for frying*
150 g sharp cheese — grated	

Combine all the patty ingredients in the order given. Mix well.

Drop the mixture a spoon at a time into hot oil and fry gently until crisp and brown on the outside. If preferred, you can give the patties more even shapes by dropping them into more flour and rolling them between the floured palms of your hands before frying.

ZUCCHINI PATTIES
Yield: 18-20 smallish patties

(14.)

These patties are a good family dish, but can also be 'tarted up' for use at a dinner party by serving them with stuffed tomatoes on top (see recipe 26).

600 g zucchini — grated	*2 pinches vegetable salt*
1 onion — grated	*4 tablespoons corn meal*
1 slice whole wheat (or rye)	*(polenta)*
bread crust — grated	*4 tablespoons arrowroot*
2 pinches dried marjoram	*4 tablespoons soy flour*
2 pinches dried sage	*40 g butter (see Butter versus*
	Margarine)

In a large bowl combine all ingredients except the butter, in the order given, mixing well. Work quickly so that the vegetables don't start giving off their juices. If this should happen, press the mixture well, drain off the liquid and keep it for soup stock.

Heat the butter in a skillet or frying pan and fry the patties gently until they are cooked and brown on both sides. Butter is better than oil for this recipe as the patties tend to stick if fried in oil.

15. GOLDEN GRAIN BALLS
Yield: 24 smallish walnut-sized balls

These balls are very easily made, are full of protein and hold together well in cooking.

2 cups cooked, drained millet
2 cups cooked, drained brown
  rice
½ cup white miso
1 clove garlic — crushed
1 teaspoon sweet red paprika
1 dessertspoon dried sage

1 good pinch dried marjoram
¼ cup finely chopped parsley
½ cup wholemeal rye flour
1 scant cup whole wheat or rye
  breadcrumbs for coating
oil for frying

Mix together the cooked grains, miso and flavourings. When they are well mixed add the rye flour. Roll into walnut-sized balls, and then roll the balls in the breadcrumbs. Fry in oil until golden.

Serve with tomato or cheese sauce (recipes 59 and 60) or just lemon juice and, of course, a tossed salad.

16. RICE BURGERS
Serves 4

Vegetarian burgers have been around for a long time and, somewhere along the way, most people have tasted them and been turned off vegetarian food, sometimes for life. They often taste like chook food, bound together with what one dares not think about, and fried. However, this recipe isn't too bad, and there are times when it's convenient to make a few burgers, e.g. when you've been invited to a barbecue by your meat-eating friends.

½ cup finely chopped parsley
1 large onion — minced
1 tablespoon kelp granules
3 heaped dessertspoons soy
  flour
2 tablespoons homemade
  Tomato Sauce (recipe 59) (or 2
  tablespoons tomato flakes and
  1 tablespoon liquid)

300 g starchy vegetables
  (parsnips, carrots, pumpkin,
  potato) — steamed and
  mashed (or 1 good cup of
  leftover vegetables — mashed)
2 cups cooked brown rice

Mix the parsley, onion, kelp, soy flour and tomato sauce well. Then add the mashed vegetables and finally the rice.

Form into patties with your floured hands and fry until heated through.

STIR FRIES

17.

The Chinese certainly know how to cook vegetables to retain their crispness and goodness. However not all they do is so good; for example, the use of MSG (monosodium glutamate) and very salty ingredients, and even white rice. However, we can adapt their stir-fried vegetables beautifully for the vegetarian diet. Kids like the opportunity of using chopsticks also. If you can put up with mishaps for a while, they soon learn to manage — as do adults.

The use of a wok is almost essential as you need to be able to stir the vegetables rapidly over a high heat and, if you use a frying pan, they plop over the sides. It's worth buying a stainless steel wok (available from Asian groceries) as ordinary steel ones go 'yukky' with food left in them and also rust easily.

Prepare all your ingredients beforehand so that they can be cooked in a minimum of time and therefore won't over cook. To describe it simply, you put a little oil and seasonings (garlic, ginger, paprika, cumin, etc.) in the wok and quickly fry your longest-to-cook vegetables, adding the other vegetables in stages and finishing with bean shoots which virtually need only stirring through to heat at the last minute. If your vegetables need more moisture, a little juice, water, vinegar or sherry can be added along the way.

If you like your vegetables coated with a sauce, mix some liquid with arrowroot and stir it in at the end to thicken the whole.

Ingredients which are suitable include most vegetables, and discards like celery leaves and broccoli stalks (sliced finely) can be used successfully. Nuts are fabulous and pineapple is nice for an occasional sweet/sour dish. My kids love Ginger Honeyed Pickles (see recipe 41) stirred through with the pickling liquid thickened for the sauce.

If you browse around Asian groceries you can discover some interesting ingredients — without having to use canned products — for adding a surprise note occasionally. There are various dried 'goodies' (e.g. fungi and lily flowers) which one hopes haven't been treated with chemicals. These need to be soaked in hot water for about 20 minutes before use.

Dried bean curd also needs to be soaked. This is an amazing product which comes in flat sheets or rolled and, after soaking, has a rubbery texture which the kids find amusing. It is certainly high in protein and can be given more flavour by soaking in a flavoured liquid, e.g. orange juice, cinnamon and cloves. The soaking liquid can then be used for the sauce.

Also fun, if of dubious dietary benefit, are pure white, very fine noodles made of mung beans. They are extremely slippery and glutinous after a few minutes' cooking. If you can put up with the sight of the kids sucking up the very long noodles one by one until they 'flip' into their mouths, it certainly makes the meal exciting for them. This can be used as leverage by mothers of real problem eaters — 'You eat the vegetables and I'll serve you noodles.'

18. MILD MEXICAN TACO MIX

Commence preparation in advance
Serves 6-8

350 g dried beans (Red kidney beans should be used for an authentic 'beany' 'earthy' flavour, but if your family doesn't like them, white cannellini beans can be substituted as they seem to have little of their own flavour.)
1 medium onion — chopped
1 clove garlic — crushed

¼ teaspoon ground cumin
2 teaspoons sweet red paprika
½ teaspoon oregano
½ cup butter (see Butter versus Margarine)
3 tablespoons dehydrated tomato flakes
12 stoned black olives — chopped
2 packets of 12 taco shells

Soak the beans overnight. Cook them the next day in a pressure cooker if you have one; otherwise boil or steam them in your usual saucepan until tender. Drain off most of the liquid for use as soup stock and retain just sufficient to mash the beans well.

Saute the onion, garlic and spices in butter for a couple of minutes and then add the tomato flakes and olive pieces. Then add the mixture to the mashed beans. Spread the resultant paste in the taco shells and line them up in a baking dish for heating in a moderate oven (180°C/350°F) for 10 minutes. Sliced tomatoes and grated cheese may be added to the taco shells at this point, but I prefer to serve the tomatoes raw. When heated serve the tacos with side dishes of shredded lettuce, grated carrot, any fresh herbs, sliced avocado, finely sliced mushrooms — indeed any raw vegetable. Then members of the family can choose their own ingredients and assemble them at the table — a boon for the kids.

FALAFEL

19.

Commence preparation in advance
Yield: 30

Falafel, or ta'amia, are spicy Middle Eastern balls or patties which seem to be always popular and are high in protein, if a bit sinful because of the deep frying.

My girls wouldn't eat cumin seeds in other food until they had had falafel a few times and developed a real taste for them.

350 g dried chickpeas	2 teaspoons ground coriander
2 large brown onions	7 tablespoons soy flour
2 large cloves garlic	pinch sea salt
100 g parsley (stalks and all)	pinch cayenne pepper
3 teaspoons ground cumin	

Soak the chickpeas overnight if possible, but for at least 6 hours. Cook until tender in the same water (which afterwards can be reserved for stock).

Mince the onions, garlic, parsley and chickpeas and then mix with the remaining ingredients in a large bowl. Form into walnut-sized balls between the palms of your hands. If you're a 'dab hand' at deep frying, you can deep fry these balls and serve them just like your local Middle Eastern restaurant. However, if you flatten the balls into patties (which is quite legit!) they are easier to fry. I prefer to shallow fry them as it's easier and healthier.

Serve them with warm flat bread, Hummus (recipe 70) and a salad containing lots of tomatoes, parsley and lemon juice. These are the main flavours of tabbouleh, the traditional Lebanese cracked wheat salad which is served with falafel, but which is a bit of a drag to make, and I find that kids don't take to it too well at first.

20. PAKORAS

Yield: see para. 2

Most 'dyed in the wool' vegetarians are aware of these sinful but scrummy Indian delights. They are a particularly tasty version of deep fried vegetables. Some batters have more in the way of hot and/or tasty spices, but kids really like this one and it is still tasty enough for adults. When Emma was in Class 5 at school they had been learning about India and had an Indian lunch which they cooked themselves (with a little adult help). The whole class took to these in a big way.

It's not possible to state the yield as it depends on how thick your batter is, how big your vegetable pieces are and how many are going to partake of it. Also, pakoras should be served with an accompanying dish (see Dhall, recipe 21). However, this makes a 'goodly quantity'.

Batter:
2 cups lentil flour (besan) or pea flour (brose meal) — available at your health food store
2 small onions — grated
2 cloves garlic — crushed
1½ teaspoons ground turmeric
1 teaspoon ground coriander
2 teaspoons ground cumin

Filling:
Any vegetables in plentiful supply which you wish to use up, although the batter doesn't stick so well to smooth firm surfaces such as carrots and broccoli stalks. Cauliflower and broccoli tops are the very best vegetables, but also tasty are potatoes, onion rings and zucchini.

Mix all the batter ingredients together well in the order given, and then add sufficient water a little at a time to form a very thick batter. Coat the vegetables and deep fry in hot oil until golden. It's no good frying them the day before as the fried batter goes soggy. However, any leftover batter will keep refrigerated for a day or two.

21. DHALL

Yield: see para. 1

As with Pakoras (recipe 20), this should not really be served alone. Even with rice you can double the number of mouths catered for, and therefore it is not possible to state the yield.

This particular Indian dish is not so popular with the kids at first. The trick I used with my kids to get them to eat dhall (which is very high in protein) was to lay out a regular feast of Indian goodies which they could partake of as long as they ate something of everything. It worked and now, when I wish to slap together a quick meal (which is most nights, I might say), I simply serve dhall and pappadums, raw tomato wedges and thick slices of banana sprinkled with shredded coconut, and sometimes steamed brown rice.

The recipe I give below is not hot, but you can zap it by adding chilli powder and cayenne if you wish. Alternatively, if you would like a spicy version, add a little cinnamon and cloves, say, half a teaspoon of each.

250 g yellow split peas (or red lentils)	*1 teaspoon ground turmeric*
1 clove garlic — crushed	*½ teaspoon ground ginger*
2 large onions — sliced	*¼ teaspoon ground coriander*
3 tablespoons oil	*500 g tomatoes and 2 or 3*
1 teaspoon ground cumin	*zucchini if you want to make it into more of a meal*

Cook the split peas or lentils until soft (about ½ hour). If using lentils wash them in a colander first to remove the 'stones'. Meanwhile, crush the garlic and slice the onions and fry them with the spices in oil. Add the cooked peas to this (and the vegetables if used) and cook for another ten minutes or so.

PASTA   22.
Yield: see para. 2

Gone are the days of preparing several sauces over a hot stove and layering them in a baking dish. This way of preparing pasta is so delicious that you wouldn't think it could be so easy if you were to taste it as my guest. You simply make Uncooked Tomato Sauce (recipe 59) and stir it through your cooked, washed and drained wholemeal macaroni. (To cook the pasta, follow the directions on the packet. Allow about a cup of uncooked noodles per person.) Then you put it in your lasagne dish and make Quick Cheese Sauce (recipe 60) and spread that over the top. Now pop it in a moderate oven (180°C/350°F) to heat through (about 20 minutes) and, hey presto! you have a scrumptious meal. If you prefer to layer the tomato sauce, you can.

You will probably have to double the quantity of Uncooked Tomato Sauce or halve the Quick Cheese Sauce. As a guide, the larger quantities with pasta will serve six or so.

Alternatively, if you enjoy puddling about in the kitchen and you want to go to more trouble, layer your lasagne with 'Bolognese' Sauce (recipe 54), Uncooked Tomato Sauce (recipe 59) and Mixed Grain Cheese Sauce (recipe 56). This is a better dish to serve your meat-eating friends as it is heavier and looks 'meaty'.

23. ZUCCHINI PASTA
Serves 4-6

This is a great way to use up zucchini when they're in your garden or cheap at the market. Emma and Mia learnt to like zucchini by my using it like this. If you need to disguise the zucchini for your kids, simply peel them, as the resulting long ribbons don't look like zucchini and the other strong Italian-type flavours easily camouflage the bland vegetable.

4 tablespoons oil
2 good sized cloves of garlic
  — crushed
2 teaspoons dried basil
2 teaspoons dried oregano
3 teaspoons sweet red paprika
1 kg zucchini — sliced
  lengthwise as finely as
  possible

100 g cheese — grated
¼-⅓ cup wholemeal flour to
  thicken (amount depends
  upon how much liquid has
  been released during cooking)
about 1 cup vegetable macaroni
  per serve

Heat the oil in a very large skillet or frying pan and gently saute the garlic with the herbs and paprika for a couple of minutes. Then turn the heat up and stir through about one-third of the zucchini. When it is coated with the oil and herbs, stir another third through and then the final third. Turn down the heat and allow to simmer until the zucchini is soft, when the grated cheese can be stirred in.

When the cheese has melted, thicken the mixture by removing a little of the juice, mixing it with flour and then stirring it in until the juice in the skillet thickens.

Meanwhile, have the pasta boiled, rinsed and drained, and served up on individual plates. Put these in a warm oven (120°C/250°F) until the zucchini topping is ready.

Serve with a crisp tossed salad which includes tomatoes and Calamata olives.

POLENTA

24.

Serves 6

This is probably the most economical meal ever devised by *wo*man. It is *so* simple and *so* tasty when served as suggested.

Since I had Peter, Mia has become a bit confused about the name of this dish and says things like, 'We're having placenta for dinner tonight.' But this hasn't altered our taste for it.

1½ cups polenta (maize or corn meal)	2 cups boiling water
	1 teaspoon sea salt
1½ cups cold water	200 g cheese — grated

Mix polenta with the cold water in a large saucepan and then add the boiling water and salt. Stir over the heat until it thickens and 'blomps'.

Remove from the heat and spread it into a very large, well oiled baking dish so that it is about ½ to 1 cm thick.

Now top it with the grated cheese and cook in a moderate (180°C/350°F) oven for half an hour or so, after which the 'custard' can be sliced and served with Uncooked Tomato Sauce (recipe 59). Put the sauce on the table along with a crisp tossed salad with olives strewn through so the kids can help themselves — yum!

More sophisticated main meals and vegetable dishes

It is really hard to know where to draw the line and decide which dishes are more sophisticated and which are not, but this is an attempt to select a few that you could use successfully when entertaining. I haven't included any of the traditional Mexican, Indian, Italian or Middle Eastern dishes here as they can be dressed up or down as circumstances dictate, e.g. a bowl of spaghetti is hardly sophisticated, and yet a dish of layered lasagne with a creamy sauce served with an elegant tossed salad can make a truly sophisticated meal.

It is, of course, always hard to be completely sophisticated with vegetarian main courses, just because of expectations, I suppose, but my hope is that the new age hostess will not be trying to emulate her mother in preparing course after course of tasty but largely dead food. Rather, she will not be afraid to use the best white china to serve simple and whole foods, and she will serve them with love and laughter because she has not had to slave all day over a hot stove.

25. CHEESE AND COCONUT MUSHROOMS
Serves 4

This is an extremely tasty dish which takes almost no time to prepare. The filling is also nice on top of other vegetables, and I have therefore given the recipe for a circle of mushrooms around other vegetables of your choice, an arrangement which looks attractive. However, if preferred, you can stick to mushrooms alone.

10-12 medium-sized mushrooms
other vegetables, e.g. carrots,
 cauliflower — sliced
1 tablespoon oil

Filling:
2 tablespoons parsley — finely
 chopped
2 cloves garlic — pressed
100 g cheese — grated (not too
 tasty)
3 tablespoons dessicated
 coconut

Clean the mushrooms, remove their stalks if desired, and place the caps around the edge of an ovenproof dish which is large enough to leave a space in the middle equivalent to, say, about another six mushrooms. (There's no need to grease the dish.)

The whole of the filling can be prepared in the food processor if you like, commencing with the parsley and garlic, then grating the cheese and finally adding the coconut for a few seconds — just sufficient to mix the whole. The resulting filling, which is a beautiful grassy green, should be patted into the upturned mushrooms, leaving enough over for dotting between layers of sliced vegetables in the centre of the dish.

These vegetables can be any you prefer, but choose from those which cook quickly or can be eaten semi-raw, as the dish will not be in the oven for long. Cauliflower and carrot are good and look good too with the bright green of the filling. Slice the vegetables about ¼ to ½ cm thick and steam for 1 minute before putting in the centre of the dish.

Sprinkle a little oil over the arranged dish to moisten it and then cook in a moderate oven (180°C/350°F) for 10-15 minutes — *no more*, as the mushrooms look terrible when overdone, apart from the loss of nutritive value of course.

Alternative:
For a more filling meal, arrange the mushrooms, etc. on a bed of cooked brown rice, millet or any other grain; 1½-2 cups should do.

BRIGHT STUFFED TOMATOES 26.

Serves 5-6

10-12 small to medium (75 to 100 g each) nicely red tomatoes
Herbed Potato Dip (recipe 74)

a little wheat germ (or millet flakes)

With a pointed, serrated knife cut out the calyx attachment of each tomato and discard. Then repeat the process taking out a little bit more of the tomato and keep these pieces for another recipe.

Now take a rounded to heaped dessertspoon of the Herbed Potato Dip and stuff each tomato with it. Sprinkle a little wheat germ on top of the bright green stuffing as garnish, arrange in an ovenproof dish and heat in a moderate oven (180°C/350°F) for 20-30 minutes. If you're using a ceramic or enamel dish there's no need to grease it.

To make this a more special dish, you can use Zucchini Patties (recipe 14) as a base. Put about half a teaspoon of Herbed Potato Dip in the centre of each cooked patty and then jam a stuffed tomato on top.

LEMON BROCCOLI

Serves 4

A most piquant dish.

1 cup raw peanuts
1 clove garlic — crushed
1 tablespoon oil

3-4 cups of flowerets and 2 cm stem pieces of broccoli — very lightly steamed
zest of half a lemon
juice of half a lemon

Fry the peanuts and garlic in the oil. When the peanuts are crunchy, toss in the broccoli pieces and lemon zest. Move them around the pan to absorb the flavour and get a coating of oil. Just before the broccoli is ready to be served, sprinkle the lemon juice over it.

28. CREAMY VEGETABLE PIE

Serves 6

This meal is one of our favourites. Emma and Mia nearly always order it when their friends are coming to dinner and it is really good to have a recipe like this which all kids seem to like and yet is appreciated by adults as well. It has a very subtle flavour and I wouldn't recommend serving it with a strongly flavoured accompaniment.

Creamy sauce:
125 g butter
125 g brown rice flour
600 ml milk or milk and water
  mixture
½ teaspoon sea salt
½ teaspoon freshly ground
  nutmeg
a grinding of black pepper and
  allspice (see Cooking Notes)
½ teaspoon mixed herbs
½ teaspoon dried sage (most
  important — do not omit)

Vegetables:
200 g carrots — diced
100 g broccoli — sliced in 1 cm
  slices
100 g whole baby mushrooms
200 g zucchini — sliced in ½ cm
  slices
100 g leeks — sliced 1 cm with
  rings pushed out

Pie crust:
enough to line and cover a
  1½ litre dish (recipe 84 or
  recipe 85)

To make the sauce, melt the butter in a large saucepan, stir in the brown rice flour and cook for a few minutes. When the roux is ready, pour in the cold milk/water (if it is not cold, add a little at a time to avoid lumps) and stir until the sauce is thickened. Season with the salt, spices and herbs. Taste and adjust the seasonings if required. Now set the sauce aside.

Steam the carrot and broccoli slices for 1 minute and then add all the vegetables to the creamy sauce. Mix well and fill the pie dish with them, cover with pastry and bake at 180°C/350°F for about 30-40 minutes until a skewer poked in the middle meets with no great resistance from the vegetables.

Serve with a very delicate tossed salad of, say, lettuce, fresh herbs and bean shoots only.

WELLINGTON PIE 29.
Serves 6-8

Mostly I don't miss eating meat — in fact, I enjoy not being weighed down by dead animal flesh. However, if I'm really honest with myself, I'll admit there are two things that I miss occasionally — shellfish and the taste of meaty gravy in pastry. It is because of this latter penchant that I have devised Wellington Pie. Of course, you will have guessed correctly that it is based on Beef Wellington. I use port instead of claret because we no longer drink alcohol and I keep a flagon of port for cooking. However, if you have claret open, please use it as the flavour is superior for this recipe.

100 g butter (see Butter versus Margarine)
a few (50-80 g) spring onions — chopped
a couple of grindings of black pepper and allspice (see Cooking Notes)
½-1 cup parsley — finely chopped
1 rounded teaspoon miso kome (see Cooking Notes)
1 average zucchini — sliced

250 g open mushrooms — sliced (or 500 g button champignons — probably nicer because of the more delicate flavour, but less economical)
½ cup port wine and 1 table-spoon arrowroot mixed together
1 kg cooked potatoes — sliced in ½ cm slices
wholemeal pie crust (recipe 84) or Non-Wheaten Pastry (recipe 85) I use a small 1½ litre baking dish (26 x 22 cm / 10 x 8½ in)

Melt the butter in a large saucepan and saute the spring onions for a couple of minutes. Add the black pepper/allspice, parsley and miso and stir until the miso has dissolved. Now add the zucchini slices and, when they are somewhat softened, add the sliced mushrooms. When the mushrooms are soft and have released their juices, thicken with the port and arrowroot mixed together.

Now take the pan off the heat and stir the potato slices through, a few at a time, to make sure they all get coated with the sauce.

Have your dish already lined with pastry.

Fill the pie and cover with a pastry lid. Bake at 200°C/400°F for 25-30 minutes until the pastry is cooked.

30. PEA POD PIE

Serves 4-6

This recipe is for sugar peas which, like their cousins the snow peas, have tender, edible pods. If you are lucky enough to have even ordinary peas growing in your own garden you can harvest them when they are very young and still have tender pods!

Wholemeal Pastry (recipe 84) or Non-Wheaten Pastry (recipe 85)
400 g sugar peas in pods
75 g butter
150 g leek — sliced
¼ teaspoon sea salt

a few grindings of black pepper and allspice (see Cooking Notes)
1 teaspoon dried sage
75 g millet meal
400 ml milk or milk and water mixture

Line a 20 cm diameter pie plate with pastry and reserve some for the top. Set aside.

Wash, top and tail the sugar peas and chop them in halves crosswise. Steam very lightly and set aside.

Melt the butter and saute the leek with the salt, pepper/allspice and herbs. When the leek is soft stir in the millet meal and cook for a couple of minutes, stirring all the while. Add the liquid (all at once if cold or in stages if not) and stir until the sauce has thickened.

Add the peas to the sauce and pour into the pastry case. Cover the pie with the remaining pastry. Bake at 200°C/400°F for 25-30 minutes until the pastry is cooked.

31. INDIAN POTATOES

Serves 6

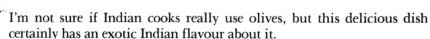

I'm not sure if Indian cooks really use olives, but this delicious dish certainly has an exotic Indian flavour about it.

1 kg potatoes
2 or 3 spring onions — finely chopped
1 clove garlic — crushed

12 stoned black olives — chopped
4 tablespoons oil
1½ teaspoons ground turmeric

Steam the washed potatoes until almost tender and then cut them into large dice or fat slices. Finely chop the spring onions, crush the garlic and stone and chop the olives.

Heat the oil in a large heavy skillet or frying pan and saute the onions, garlic and turmeric until the onions are soft. Then add the olives and potatoes and fry until the potatoes are a little crisp outside.

FRIED POTATO BALLS 32.

Serves 6

I don't fry food often; especially I avoid deep frying (which is easier for this recipe), as too much oil hinders the digestion, while high heat destroys vitamins and apparently renders the oil cancer forming. However, 'a little in moderation' is a good rule which served our forefathers well.

1 kg potatoes
½ cup wheat germ (or millet flakes)
½ cup wholemeal wheat (or rye) flour
more flour for coating
oil for deep frying

herbs and spices to taste (This recipe is good with any of the following: caraway seeds, celery seeds, cumin seeds, crushed garlic, finely chopped spring onions, grated lemon rind, mustard, grated cheese, kelp granules, mint, parsley.)

Wash and steam the potatoes and, when cooked, mash without liquid. Mix in remaining ingredients and then take more flour and sprinkle it over the top of the potato mix.

Pinch off pieces of the mixture and drop into another saucer of flour. Roll the pieces into balls between your floured palms and deep fry in hot oil for about 5 minutes. Drain and serve hot, or else cool and then serve.

These potato balls can't be kept overnight. If you wish to keep some of the mixture for use later on in a salad, why not roll out little balls and freeze them until the day they're needed. Then defrost and fry them in time to allow them to cool.

33. RICE BALLS
Serves 4

This is one of my more fiddly or messy recipes, which I normally keep for visitors rather than the family. But don't be put off; it is as easy as falling off a log, and easier than a pie.

Balls:
6 cups cooked brown rice   *2 tablespoons unsalted peanut*
(refrigerated and sticky)   *butter*
1 tablespoon kelp granules

Don't rinse the rice after it has been cooked; the stickier it is, the better for forming into balls. It is also easier to use if it is quite cold.

Mix the kelp and peanut butter thoroughly into the rice.

Filling:
(enough for about two rounded   *80 g (1 good cup) celery tops —*
tablespoons for each ball)   *finely chopped*
60 g cheese — grated   *25 g (¼-⅓ cup) roasted unsalted*
50 g onion (½ a small onion) —   *peanuts*
very finely chopped

Thoroughly mix filling ingredients.

Coating:
about ½ cup wheat germ (may be substituted by millet meal if you have a wheat allergy).

To assemble:
Make some of the rice into a nest in the palm of your hand. Put two rounded tablespoons of the filling into the nest and mould more rice over the top to make an apple-sized ball with the filling in the middle. Compress it well. Roll the ball in wheat germ. Then make the other balls in the same way. When all the balls are ready, fry them slowly in oil until the fillings are warmed through and they are crisp on the outside. However, if, like me, you're a lousy frier, put them in a baking dish in the oven (190°C/375°F) in a little oil, rolling them over from time to time.

Delicious served with Uncooked Tomato Sauce (recipe 59).

34. TOFU KEBABS
Commence preparation in advance

Tofu cubes skewered with vegetables and pineapple are another handy item for a barbecue.

Tofu is a wonderful source of protein, but it is rather bland! I suggest therefore you marinate it. The marinade below is very tasty, and, as long as your children like the flavour of it, they are sure to like tofu prepared like this. As the first impression can often be a lasting one, why not thicken the marinade and try it out as a sauce on a known and loved food? Then the transfer of taste will be simply achieved.

Before marinating the tofu, it must be pressed for a couple of hours to get out much of its moisture. Put it on the sink with kitchen paper and a chopping board on top, and then put a weighty pot or iron on top of that.

By the way, almonds are delicious when 'devilled' by soaking in this marinade. Cut them in halves lengthwise and drop them into the space around the tofu. Then drain and fry them and serve them as a side dish, or a garnish on a rice bed, for example.

Marinade:
This is enough for up to 750 g tofu if you use a soaking vessel not much bigger than the tofu block, e.g. a lunch box or an old fashioned rectangular enamel pie dish.

⅓ cup Herbed Apple Cider
  Vinegar (recipe 146)
⅔ cup water
1 tablespoon soy sauce
1 clove garlic — crushed
1 teaspoon ground ginger

1 teaspoon cumin seeds —
  ground or partly ground
a couple of grindings of black
  pepper and allspice (see
  Cooking Notes)
1 heaped teaspoon Honey
  Mustard (recipe 139)

Mix up the above ingredients, in the order given, and stand the tofu in the marinade for at least 12 hours, longer if possible. Finally, before you grill the tofu, sit it in a colander for about another half an hour to drain off the excess liquid. (Don't press it this time.)

To make kebabs, the tofu should be cut into large dice and pushed onto skewers (cheap bamboo ones are available from Asian groceries) with a variety of fruit and vegetable pieces which are good grilled and eaten fairly crisp. Pineapple, peppers, firm tomatoes and zucchini are all good. You'll need to avoid things which are so crisp that they crack apart when skewered. The kebabs can be grilled on a hotplate or under the griller, or even fried in a very little oil.

Serve the kebabs as they are or, for a more substantial meal, on a bed of rice.

If you like you can thicken the marinade with about a teaspoon of arrowroot and serve it as an accompaniment to the kebabs.

You may prefer to use the marinated tofu cubes with stir fried vegetables, in which case, stir the marinade and arrowroot through the vegetables in the wok at the last moment. Alternatively, you can serve your tofu in strips on the plate with the marinade thickened as gravy — just like the old meat and three veg. days!

35. FESTIVE NUT RING WITH CHERRY SAUCE

Serves 6

People had warned me that books drag on and on before getting to the point where they can be published. The night before my final deadline with the publishers was to expire (having missed a few already), I was asked by members of The Melbourne Therapy Centre for Cancer and Other Patients to provide a recipe for Christmas dinner for their forthcoming December newsletter. Christmas dinner has always presented a bit of a problem for vegetarians. They don't know whether to have baked vegetables and stuffing and go for the traditional flavours of Christmas without the dead bird bit, or whether to make a complete change and serve a pie or casserole. Some people I know eat flesh on Christmas Day, and at no other time of the year, just because of this dilemma — but, to my mind, Christmas Day is the very day when one *shouldn't* eat God's creatures!

Anyway, back to the Therapy Centre's requirements. I remembered a friend had supplied me with a recipe for a brazil nut ring roast years ago and I told them that that might do the trick but, when I looked it up, I found it was literally dripping with tomatoes and tomato juice. Now, the Therapy Centre, being based on Rudolf Steiner's philosophies, recommends that everyone, and cancer patients in particular, avoid tomatoes and potatoes, as they are both members of the nightshade family, a poisonous plant strain. So this recipe wouldn't do at all. Well, I substituted and added, and, although I say so myself, the result is better than the original, and certainly more Christmassy in flavour.

So this then delayed the book some more, but it supplied an otherwise missing element to my menus.

Nut Ring:

1 teaspoon butter (see Butter versus Margarine)

2 tablespoons fine dry breadcrumbs

800 g zucchini — steamed in as little water as possible

1 average brown onion — finely chopped

200 g Brazil nuts — freshly ground

150 g fresh breadcrumbs, wholemeal wheat (or rye)

2 tablespoons soy flour

4 tablespoons milk powder (or soy milk powder)

2 tablespoons rolled oats

2 teaspoons good dried mixed herbs

½ teaspoon sea salt

Pre-heat the oven to 190°C/375°F.

Grease a ring mould with the butter and sprinkle the dry breadcrumbs over it to coat the surfaces evenly, shaking off any excess into the compost bin. Alternatively, the finished product is firm enough to stand alone if you don't have a ring mould or if you want to make a larger hole in the centre; so you can use any baking dish or pie dish and 'sculpt' the ring on it. Set the ring mould or baking dish aside and mix the ingredients.

Mash the zucchini well (you should end up with 3 cups of pulp) and then mix in all the remaining ingredients.

Fill the ring mould or 'sculpt' your own ring and bake it for 50 minutes or until a knife inserted into the middle comes out clean.

Remove the ring from the oven and allow it to cool a little, for, say, 5 minutes. Now loosen the ring with a knife and hold a warm serving platter above it. Invert, holding the two firmly together, sit the serving dish on the bench and lift off the baking dish.

Fill the centre with steamed vegetables, say, baby carrots and beans, and serve with baked pumpkin and parsnip and cold Cherry Sauce.

Cherry Sauce:
Take the recipe for Port and Fruit Sauce (recipe 67) and substitute the fruit of 125 g of fresh juicy cherries for the dried fruit.

Everything else is the same, except you won't need to leave the fruit to soak overnight — twenty minutes will be enough — and you also won't need to thin the sauce at all, as you will end up with two cups of sauce of just the right consistency.

26 more ideas for main meals for the more experienced cook

A. Cooked brown rice and beans (any sort — black eye, red kidney, soy, etc.) with Peanut Sauce (recipe 52) and steamed vegetables.

B. Pizzas made on any bread spread with Uncooked Tomato Sauce (recipe 59) and topped with any very finely sliced vegetables (broccoli, cabbage, cauliflower, celery, mushrooms, zucchini) and bean shoots. Then add the usual pizza trappings — peppers and olives — if you like and finally top with cheese. Bake in a moderate oven until the bread is warmed, the vegetables soft and the cheese melted.

C. Avocado slices fanned on a bed of brown rice and served with Mandarin Orange Sauce (recipe 61) and salad.

D. Cooked beans served Italian style, e.g., with Uncooked Tomato Sauce (recipe 59) and Quick Cheese Sauce (recipe 60). Serve with tossed salad.

E. Roast potatoes, parsnip, pumpkin, etc., with Herbed Apple and Prune Sauce (recipe 53) and salad.

F. Roast root vegetables, steamed greens and Port and Fruit Sauce (recipe 67).

G. Casserole of beans and vegetables with tomatoes and typically Italian flavours, e.g., garlic, olives, oregano, peppers, sweet basil. Cover the top with breadcrumbs or wheat germ and cheese.

H. Casserole of beans and vegetables with Middle Eastern flavours which include: coriander and cumin; cinnamon and ginger; garlic or onions; lemon juice, parsley and mint; yoghurt, raisins and pine nuts. Serve with brown rice and nuts.

I. Fondue: make a cheese sauce using the roux method and serve bowls of large croutons, raw vegetable chunks and maybe marinated tofu squares (recipe 34) for dipping.

J. Wholemeal macaroni and vegetable casserole.

K. Vegetable rolls: thicken with arrowroot some finely chopped, seasoned and sauteed vegetables. When the mixture has cooled a little, wrap it in (white!) spring roll skins (pastry) available at Asian groceries. These are supposed to be deep fried, but I feel happier roasting them in just a little oil and turning them over so that two sides are brown. Make sure, though, that they do not touch each other in the dish as the sides will stick together and tear away when moved.

L. Butternut pumpkin stuffed with rice and Port and Fruit Sauce (recipe 67). Serve with steamed vegetables.

M. Red peppers (or tomatoes if your family doesn't like peppers) stuffed with marinated tofu (recipe 34) and nuts, with the marinade thickened as a sauce. Serve with salads.

N. Zucchini stuffed with small dice of tofu and Peanut Sauce (recipe 52). Serve with Carrot Salad (recipe 45) and/or Sweet Ginger Pickle Salad (recipe 40).

O. Pre-steamed small beetroot stuffed with ground nuts and Herbed Apple and Prune Sauce (recipe 53). Serve with salads.

P. Pastry rounds (roll out your excess pastry, cook it and freeze until you have enough for a meal) with steamed vegetables and Mushroom Sauce (recipe 55).

Q. Pastry rounds topped with Herbed Potato Dip (recipe 74) and heated in the oven. Serve with a tomato, zucchini and onion dish and tossed salad.

R. Good old fashioned pasties (without the meat, of course).

S. Cooked brown lentils and cubes of marinated tofu (recipe 34) with the marinade thickened as a sauce, with pineapple pieces, chopped tomatoes and sliced Chinese cabbage stirred through while heating.

T. Hot finger foods: heat some Middle Eastern bread and a couple of traditional Middle Eastern spreads. Hummus (recipe 70) is particularly liked by kids. Serve with flowerets of broccoli, celery sticks and tomato wedges, all of which can be dipped. They also form a lovely contrast with the bread and pastes.

U. Cheese tarts: wholemeal pastry (recipe 84) topped with Mixed Grain Cheese Sauce (recipe 56). Add finely sliced vegetables which will cook through as the pastry cooks.

V. Mushroom tarts: wholemeal pastry (recipe 84) topped with Mushroom Sauce (recipe 55).

W. Pizza topping placed on a thin bed of cooked brown rice (leave the rice unwashed for better adhesion). For easier serving, put the cheese directly onto the rice and then the other ingredients on top of the cheese.

X. Hot potato salad: steam your potatoes and then cut them into very large dice while still hot. Have ready beforehand a homemade dressing (see recipes under Blender Sauces) with fresh chopped herbs and spring onions stirred through. Quickly pour the mayonnaise over the potato dice and serve as the main component of a meal.

Y. Asparagus rolls: roll fat asparagus stalks in cheese dough (recipe 89) and bake in a moderate oven. Good for parties too.

Z. Lightly steamed vegetables rolled in wholemeal pancakes with cheese: the pancakes themselves can be flavoured with garlic and/or herbs. Arrange these 'vegetable rolls' in a shallow baking dish and dot the tops with butter or alternatively cover with a sauce, e.g. Uncooked Tomato Sauce (recipe 59). Heat in a moderate oven.

Salads

I place as much emphasis on salads as on any other dish in our diet. Most of our meals are a starch staple, served one way or another, with salad. Sometimes, we have just a big plate of salad (with exciting goodies in it). There was a time when the kids weren't too struck on salads, but now, because of the habit no doubt, they miss them. If they go to stay with friends who are not health conscious for a couple of days, as soon as we are out of earshot after collecting them, they say, 'Oh Mummy, I can't wait to have some lettuce and tomato and bean shoots or just *any*thing like that. My body feels as though it will die without them.' (My daughters are a bit on the dramatic side, but you get the general picture — their bodies miss the vitamins and minerals they are accustomed to.) In fact, when they stay with some friends they eat more than when they are at home, and we all attribute that to the fact that they, on the whole, serve their vegetables well and truly cooked.

If you can gradually wean your family onto salads, and then onto not much more than salads, you will all be healthier and you will spend much less time in the kitchen and much less money in the supermarket. (You can't eat as much raw vegetable as cooked!)

I do hope you will experiment with salads and gradually serve more and more to accompany the foods to which the family is accustomed, so that the kids gradually become used to raw vegetables and then *need* them just like mine do. Society must benefit from this — my daughters, Emma and Mia, now aged twelve and eleven, have had antibiotics four times and once respectively in their lives. Also, have you noticed how many teenaged shop assistants have the jitters when they hand you the change! This is a sign of lack of magnesium and the B group vitamins, of which they are not getting enough in their diets, and which coffee, alcohol and cola drinks destroy.

LEAFY SALAD

36.

There are so many diversions in this salad that one tends not to notice the spinach! Anyway, raw spinach is much nicer than cooked.

1 cup very finely sliced spinach leaf — well washed and dried
1 cup pale celery tops (can include some stalk) — also finely sliced and washed
1 cup alfalfa sprouts
3-4 medium tomatoes — finely sliced

½ cup finely chopped parsley
a few stoned Calamata olives — chopped
ground cumin seed (if liked)
Garlic and Herb Dressing (recipe 64)
½ cup cheese cubes

Toss vegetables in the dressing with a sprinkling of ground cumin if liked and then fold through the cheese.

PISTACHIO RICE SALAD

37.

Lots of protein here, if that's your beef (ha ha!).

1 cup Australian gouda cheese cubes
3 cups cooked brown rice
½ cup unsalted pistachio nuts — shelled

½ cup roughly chopped watercress
½ cup sliced French beans
½ cup diced carrots
¼ cup sliced celery

Dress with Tangy Day-Old Dressing (recipe 62) or Lemon and Caraway Dressing (recipe 65).

NUTTY BROCCOLI SALAD

38.

½ cup almonds
½ cup raw cashews
¼ cup shredded coconut
100 g snow peas — roughly chopped

300 g broccoli — finely sliced
150 g tomato wedges
French Dressing (recipe 58)

39. *TOMATO COLESLAW*

3 tomatoes — sliced
¼ cabbage — finely sliced
½ cucumber — finely sliced
½ cup roughly chopped
  watercress

½ cup finely sliced aniseed bulb
(fennel) (can be omitted or
white onion could be
substituted)

Dress with Tomato/Ricotta Dressing (recipe 68).

40. *SWEET GINGER PICKLE SALAD*

If the Chinese made salad, this would be it.

1 cup Ginger Honeyed Pickles
  (recipe 141)
1 cup finely sliced cauliflower
2 cups finely sliced Chinese
  cabbage

2 cups mung bean shoots
½ cup finely sliced mushrooms
1 cup grated carrot

Dress with Garlic and Herb Dressing (recipe 64) mixed with liquid from the pickles.

41. *TOMATO RICE SALAD*

Make sure that you slice the broccoli quite finely, although not nearly as finely as you would the parsley. Raw broccoli seems a bit of a mouthful, but you'll soon get to like it better than cooked broccoli. When it's raw it doesn't have that awful pong — and, of course, it is so much better for you.

3 cups cooked brown rice
1½ cups chopped broccoli

½ cup finely chopped parsley
½ cup finely sliced mushrooms

Dress with Tomato/Ricotta Dressing (recipe 68).

42. *HERBED TOMATO SALAD*

500 g finely sliced tomatoes
200 g sliced French beans

½ cup finely chopped fresh
herbs (use any or all of the
following: lemon balm, mint
and parsley)

It's really sufficient to dress this salad with only a little oil, as the tomatoes make quite a lot of acidy juice. Also, if you use lemon balm as one of your herbs that gives the tang usually supplied by lemon or vinegar in the dressing.

BEETROOT SALAD 43.

This may not appeal to all, but beetroot lovers will be delighted.

3 cups shredded raw beetroot
1 orange (finely slice the zest of
half of it; then peel it all and
chop up all the fruit)

½ teaspoon ground cloves

Dress with:

2 tablespoons cold pressed
vegetable oil

1 tablespoon Herbed Apple
Cider Vinegar (recipe 146)
1 cup yoghurt

mixed together.

ORANGE AND ANISEED SALAD 44.

This will certainly not appeal to all. However, some kids really like the flavour of aniseed.

1 average sized aniseed bulb
(fennel) — finely sliced

zest of half an orange — finely
chopped
2 oranges — finely sliced

Sprinkle over it a little oil and vinegar mixed ⅔ oil to ⅓ vinegar.

CARROT SALAD 45.

Most kids like these flavours very much, and the recipe is simple enough for them to make themselves.

2 cups shredded carrots
1 cup shelled peas

½ cup finely chopped mint

Dress with Orange Cream Dressing (recipe 63) or Mint Salad Cream (recipe 66).

46. *NOODLES AND CHEESE STICKS*

Kids hardly know they're eating vegetables with this one. The Cheese Stick pieces are very useful in trying to get the children to eat more wholesome goodies.

*200 g wholemeal macaroni —
cooked, rinsed and cooled*
1 cup sliced French beans
2 cups diced carrots

*¼ cup finely sliced spring
onions*
½ cucumber — peeled and diced
1 cup bean sprouts
*Cheese Sticks — broken (recipe
89)*

Dress with Tomato/Ricotta Dressing (recipe 68) and add the Cheese Stick pieces at the last moment to ensure their crispness.

47. *TOMATO NOODLE SALAD*

4 ripe tomatoes — chopped
½ cup of your favourite olives
*1 pepper — sliced (may be
omitted if your children don't
like it; the salad still tastes
good enough for adults)*

1 cup sliced cauliflower
*1 250 g packet cooked, rinsed
and cooled vegetable and
semolina macaroni noodles*

Dress with Uncooked Tomato Sauce (recipe 59).

48. *CHEESEY RICE SALAD*

Wandering Jew is used in this recipe — it makes a great party trick to wait for everyone to have a mouthful of salad and then announce that they are eating the indoor plants. Actually, Wandering Jew is quite good for you, especially if you have it growing outdoors where it can get all the good vibrations from the sun. Use only the top two leaves as the bigger ones are a little bitter.

4 cups cooked brown rice
2 cups bean shoots
2 cups raw cauliflower flowerets
4 medium tomatoes — chopped
2 sticks celery — sliced

½ cup finely chopped parsley
*½ green pepper (if liked) —
finely chopped*
*½ cup roughly chopped
Wandering Jew leaves*

Dress with half the quantity of Quick Cheese Sauce (recipe 60).

Three kid-tempting tossed salads

People always like my tossed salads, even meat and three veg. people whose salad intake normally consists of shredded lettuce with condensed milk dressing and tomato, cucumber and onion slices floating in vinegar on a hot Sunday night with leftover roast.

The main secret to success is the colour combination. This may sound a bit far-fetched, but picture in your mind's eye a plain bowl of lettuce and tomato, and now picture the same bowl with dark green herbs tossed through. How much fresher and more inviting does the latter appear! A tossed salad, of course, has lettuce green as its basis and *always* has to have at least one very dark green ingredient. (This is all I use for the family quite often, especially if we are to have a main course like a pasty or something with a big mix of ingredients.) The other colours which can be used are white, red and brown (or black) olives.

Perhaps your family doesn't like salad whatever its colour? Then try hiding much loved goodies amongst the tolerated ones. Fried croutons are the favourites in our household, but you can use nuts, cheese cubes, pickles, gherkins, olives, potato balls or cheese balls. Three examples follow — you'll be able to think of many more combinations yourself.

I won't give exact quantities for these salads, as you know how much salad your family will eat and, unlike other salads, tossed salads will not keep. I allow about one large lettuce leaf per head, although I would use more if I had only two or three other ingredients in it. You'll also know how much of the other goodies to use if you judge by whether the colours look well balanced.

TOSSED SALAD WITH CROUTONS 49.

lettuce — torn
parsley — finely chopped
Chinese cabbage — chopped
roughly (Use the top half of
the leaf only and keep the
bottom for stir fries (recipe 17)
or other uses)

broccoli — finely sliced
whole wheat (or rye) bread —
diced and fried with garlic and
sesame seeds
French Dressing (recipe 58)

Mix the dressing well. Pour a little (probably about half a teaspoon per serving) onto the salad, which should be in a large bowl to allow room for tossing. Take your salad spoon and fork and dig them into the salad and toss the leaves up a little, as though you're looking for something at the bottom of the bowl. Repeat this process until the leaves are fairly evenly coated with dressing.

50. *TOSSED SALAD WITH A GREEK TOUCH*

*lettuce — torn (use two
  varieties)
ripe tomatoes
Calamata olives
fetta cheese cubes*

*parsley — finely chopped
green pepper — sliced in rings
cucumber with skin on —finely
  sliced
French Dressing (recipe 58)*

Mix the dressing well. Pour a little (probably about half a teaspoon per serving) onto the salad, which should be in a large bowl to allow room for tossing. Take your salad spoon and fork and dig them into the salad and toss the leaves up a little, as though you're looking for something at the bottom of the bowl. Repeat this process until the leaves are fairly evenly coated with dressing.

51. *TOSSED SALAD WITH POTATO BALLS*

*Fried Potato Balls (recipe 32)
lettuce — torn
fresh lemon balm or lemon
  thyme — finely chopped*

*snow peas
mushrooms — sliced
French Dressing (recipe 58)*

Mix the dressing well. Pour a little (probably about half a teaspoon per serving) onto the salad, which should be in a large bowl to allow room for tossing. Take your salad spoon and fork and dig them into the salad and toss the leaves up a little, as though you're looking for something at the bottom of the bowl. Repeat this process until the leaves are fairly evenly coated with dressing.

Toss the potato balls in at the last minute to retain their crispness.

Sauces and Dressings

The following sauces — some hot, some cold — are simple and can be served on all hot steamed vegetables. Wherever it is possible for a vegetable to be eaten raw, I prefer to do so, but I must say that there is nothing quite as delectable as steamed asparagus with 'Hollandaise' Sauce, except perhaps cooked broccoli with Peanut Sauce!

Do make sure that green vegetables are barely steamed — so that they are still bright green — to retain their crunchiness and, of course, lots of the vitamins for which they are famous.

52. *PEANUT SAUCE*

Yield: 2 cups

This is just so yummy that you will be serving it with anything and everything.

Raw peanuts are best, although if you have only cooked ones they will suffice, but they're not nearly as good in this recipe. You need less butter if you use cooked peanuts. Make sure, though, whatever peanuts you use, that they are freshly crushed.

100 g butter (see Butter versus Margarine)
1 clove garlic — crushed or very finely chopped
1 smallish piece (say 2 cm long) of root ginger — crushed or very finely chopped (can be omitted if not liked)

150 g raw peanuts — freshly ground
250 ml milk or other liquid (water is okay and a dash of sherry in the water jazzes it up)

Melt the butter in a medium-sized saucepan and saute the garlic and ginger. When they are a little softened stir in the crushed peanuts.

At first it will take a bit of stirring to stop the mixture from sticking. The coating which does stick to the pan will loosen after a while, when the stirring also becomes easier.

If you are using raw peanuts it may take 10 minutes over a low heat to cook them sufficiently to taste good and nutty. Cooked peanuts simply need to be warmed through — they are quicker but, as I said before, not nearly so tasty.

Now add the liquid. At first it seems as though you have too much liquid, but the sauce thickens after a bit.

53. *HERBED APPLE AND PRUNE SAUCE*

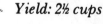
Yield: 2½ cups

1 brown onion — finely sliced
1 tablespoon butter (see Butter versus Margarine)
1 teaspoon mixed herbs

6-10 large prunes — stoned and chopped
2 or 3 cooking apples — sliced or grated

Finely chop the onion and saute in butter with the mixed herbs.

Stone and chop the prunes and add them, with the apples (sliced or grated as you prefer), to the onions and herbs.

Add a drop or two of water if necessary, cover and cook gently until the apples are soft.

'BOLOGNESE' SAUCE

54.

Yield: 3 cups

This is an incredibly 'meaty' looking sauce and is just the thing for layering with lasagne to trick Auntie Flo.

50 g butter (see Butter versus Margarine)
1 medium onion — chopped
1-2 cloves garlic — finely chopped
2 teaspoons sweet red paprika
½ teaspoon dried oregano
½ teaspoon dried basil
½ teaspoon sea salt
1½ cups cooked red kidney beans (about 100 g dried)

¾ cup cooked brown rice
12 stoned black olives — chopped
3 tablespoons dehydrated tomato flakes
2 cups liquid (from cooking the beans or the rice or use vegetable stock or just plain water)

In a largish saucepan melt the butter and saute the onion and garlic until soft. Add the spices, herbs and salt and then the kidney beans and rice. Next stir in the olive pieces, the tomato flakes and the liquid. Simmer, stirring often, for a few minutes.

Mash the sauce until it is the consistency of Bolognese sauce. (The rice won't mash, of course, and, because of the kidney bean and tomato colours, it looks very like minced steak.)

If you want to put carrot and celery in the sauce, chop or slice them. Then add them at the same time as the beans and simmer for a little longer. I don't add them to this sauce, preferring to eat as much raw vegetable as possible.

55. MUSHROOM SAUCE

Yield: 3½ cups (using 1 cup liquid)

In my carnivorous days I used to add fried bacon pieces to mushroom sauce for a contrast in flavour and texture. This sauce is very nice by itself but, if you care to fry slivers of tofu (150 g) in 1 tablespoon of hot oil and then pour soy sauce over the cooked slivers, you can achieve that contrast without the use of a part of a dead pig. Make sure you stir in the tofu 'chips' just before serving to ensure they retain some crispness.

1 large brown onion — finely chopped
a few grindings of black pepper and allspice (see Cooking Notes)
2 tablespoons butter (see Butter versus Margarine)
⅛ teaspoon sea salt
300 g mushrooms — finely sliced
1 tablespoon lemon juice

200 g Asian tofu (see Cooking Notes)
¼ cup wholemeal flour (or brown rice flour)
milk or vegetable stock or wine/water mixture

Optional extra:
150 g tofu in slivers as described above
1 tablespoon oil
2 tablespoons soy sauce

Saute the onion in the butter with the seasonings. When the onion is soft add the mushrooms and cook until they are soft.

Mix well or blend the lemon juice, tofu and flour and pour over the onion and mushroom mixture. Stir until the sauce thickens. Add milk or other liquid to bring to the desired consistency.

Add tofu slivers if desired.

MIXED GRAIN CHEESE SAUCE 56.
Yield: 5½ cups

This thick hearty sauce is almost a meal in itself. Maize flour can be substituted for the semolina if you have a wheat allergy.

75 g butter
1 large brown onion — finely
chopped
1 teaspoon dried herbs to taste
(Sage is nice but won't
necessarily go with whatever
meal you have planned — so
please yourself.)

75 g brown rice flour
25 g wholemeal rye flour
50 g semolina
800 ml milk or soy milk
200 g tasty cheese — grated

Melt the butter in a largish saucepan and add the onion and herbs. Saute the onion until soft.

Now add the flours, stir them in with a wooden spoon and keep stirring for a couple of minutes.

If the liquid is really cold, pour it in all at once. Otherwise, pour in a little at a time to avoid lumps forming. Stir until the sauce thickens and then stir in the cheese until it melts.

'HOLLANDAISE' SAUCE 57.
Yield: 1¼ cups

A true Hollandaise sauce is made with eggs, of course, but this version is very close to the real thing and is actually much easier to make. It is wonderful served hot on green vegetables, especially steamed asparagus.

75 g butter
2 tablespoons buckwheat flour
2½ tablespoons lemon juice

¼ cup water
½ cup milk
1 teaspoon dried tarragon
(optional)

Melt the butter in a small saucepan and then stir in the buckwheat flour. Heat until it bubbles and then cook for a couple of minutes, stirring all the while.

Add the liquids and stir again until a smooth texture results. Add the tarragon if you are using it. Serve hot.

58. FRENCH DRESSING

Recipes for French dressing vary as far as the flavourings go, but they all seem to be consistent in using twice as much oil as vinegar or lemon juice.

Take a jar with a well fitting screw-top plastic lid. Mentally note the one-third mark and fill up to there with Herbed Apple Cider Vinegar (recipe 146) or lemon juice or a combination of both. Then fill the remaining two-thirds with cold pressed vegetable oil. Actually, you need a little headroom to allow for shaking and spices to go in, so don't quite fill the jar.

I add a couple of teaspoons of Honey Mustard (recipe 139), a teaspoonful of kelp granules and a bruised clove of garlic to my dressing. If you fancy a sweet dressing, drop a little honey or maple syrup in. Any herbs can be added, fresh or dry. These are especially important if you haven't used Herbed Apple Cider Vinegar.

As soon as the jar is shaken vigorously the dressing is ready to use, but it will probably be nicer after a day or so when the flavours have had time to penetrate the oil better. Don't use too much (probably about a teaspoon per serving) and don't dress your tossed salad in advance, as it goes slimy and yuk. Put your jar in the refrigerator and it will keep for weeks and weeks, but, if it does, you'll know you're not eating enough salad.

Blender sauces

59. UNCOOKED TOMATO SAUCE
Yield: 1¾ cups

What a tasty treat — and to think it is all good for you! You can feel it doing you good while you're enjoying it; just the way all food should be.

300 g tomatoes, preferably very ripe	1 clove garlic
2 teaspoons dried basil	⅓ cup cold pressed vegetable oil

Put the tomato, basil and garlic in the food processor and process until smooth. Then add the oil while still processing.

The sauce will thicken on standing.

QUICK CHEESE SAUCE
60.

Yield: 3 cups

This is a versatile sauce. It can be used as it is when assembling a dish of pasta or anything to be re-heated, but it must be heated slowly or else it will curdle. If you would like to serve it hot over vegetables, heat it over a low heat. It is also good as a base for a dip in this raw state.

250 g cheese	1 teaspoon sweet red paprika
250 g Asian tofu (see Cooking Notes)	pinch cayenne pepper (if desired)
100 g cream cheese	½ cup water

Grate (or perhaps I should say pulverise) the cheese in the food processor with the metal blade in place. Add the tofu and continue processing, then the cream cheese and seasonings, and finally the water.

MANDARIN ORANGE SAUCE
61.

Yield: 1¼ cups

A most elegant and subtle cold sauce or mayonnaise. Wonderful for avocado or barely steamed cauliflower or zucchini. Garnish with chopped spring onion if liked.

100 g Asian tofu (see Cooking Notes)	1 teaspoon pure orange essence (may be omitted if zest is used)
1½ tablespoons orange juice (plus the pulp)	pinch sea salt
orange zest from about a 1 cm strip of the orange (may be omitted if not liked)	½ teaspoon honey
	1 mandarin (½ an orange may be substituted, but is not nearly so good)
½ teaspoon dried sage	¼ cup cold pressed vegetable oil

With the metal blade in place in the food processor, process the tofu, orange juice, zest, seasonings and honey until smooth. Also use some of the pulp caught around the squeezer after juicing the orange.

Cut the peeled mandarin in halves crosswise to facilitate the removal of the pips and then put it in the processor also.

Finally, pour in the oil steadily while the processor is on.

62. *TANGY DAY-OLD DRESSING*
Commence preparation in advance
Yield: 1⅓ cups

As the name implies, this dressing should be used the day after it is made, as the flavours will have integrated nicely by then.

*125 g Asian tofu (see Cooking
  Notes)
2 tablespoons very herby
  Herbed Apple Cider Vinegar
  (recipe 146) (or else add a few
  herbs to taste if your vinegar is
  a little on the dull side)*

*1 scant teaspoon ground ginger
1 scant teaspoon caraway seeds
  (not essential if not liked)
1 rounded tablespoon lecithin
  granules
1 teaspoon honey*

Blend all ingredients until smooth and place in a screw-top jar in the refrigerator. Shake vigorously before use next day.

63. *ORANGE CREAM DRESSING*
Yield: 2 cups

This dressing is also excellent as a dip. If I leave a bowl of it near my friend Jo, it is not around for very long — she eats it just as it is.

*½ clove garlic
175 g cottage cheese
2 heaped teaspoons Honey
  Mustard (recipe 139)
4 tablespoons freshly squeezed
  orange juice*

*1 tablespoon Herbed Apple
  Cider Vinegar (recipe 146)
4 tablespoons milk
1 tablespoon cold pressed
  vegetable oil*

Place the garlic in the processor and process for a few seconds with the metal blade in place. Now put in the cottage cheese and Honey Mustard and, while processing, add the liquids and blend until smooth.

64. *GARLIC AND HERB DRESSING*
Yield: 1½ cups

A simple dressing which can also be used as a dip.

1 handful of fresh oregano
  leaves
1-2 cloves of garlic, depending
  on personal taste

1 average lemon — peeled and
  roughly chopped
250 g Asian tofu (see Cooking
  Notes)
50-60 g butter (see Butter versus
  Margarine)

Throw the washed herbs and the garlic into the processor with the metal blade in place and finely chop. Now add the lemon flesh and pulverise it. Finally, the tofu and the butter can be added and blended until smooth.

If preferred, 50 g butter will be sufficient, although the larger amount is creamier.

LEMON AND CARAWAY DRESSING   65.
Yield: 1½ cups

Another simple and versatile dressing sauce.

1 average lemon — peeled and
  roughly chopped
250 g Asian tofu (see Cooking
  Notes)

2 teaspoons caraway seeds
50-60 g butter (see Butter versus
  Margarine)

Pulverise the lemon flesh in the blender or processor and then add the remaining ingredients and continue blending till smooth.

If preferred, 50 g butter will be sufficient, although the larger amount makes the dressing creamier.

MINT SALAD CREAM   66.
Yield: 2 cups

1 overflowing handful of fresh
  mint leaves
300 g cottage cheese
3 tablespoons cold pressed
  vegetable oil

1 tablespoon Herbed Apple
  Cider Vinegar (recipe 146)
2 tablespoons water or milk
1 dessertspoon honey

Finely chop the mint leaves in the blender or processor and then add the cottage cheese and blend until smooth. Next add the remaining ingredients and blend once more.

67. *PORT AND FRUIT SAUCE*

Commence preparation in advance
Yield: 2½ cups (if thinned with ½ cup liquid)

For this sauce choose whichever dried fruit you fancy to suit the meal. Pears are superb, vine fruits marvellous and apricots very good.

75 g dried fruit
⅜ cup port
⅜ cup water
200 g Asian tofu (see Cooking Notes)

1 pinch dried oregano
1 pinch dried marjoram
¼ cup cold pressed vegetable oil
25 g onion greens — chopped
⅛ teaspoon sea salt

Chop the dried fruit roughly and bring to the boil with the port and water. Simmer for three to four minutes and leave to soak, preferably overnight, but at least two hours.

Blend the soaked fruit mixture and the tofu and then add the remaining ingredients.

Thin with water to achieve the desired consistency. Half a cup still leaves the sauce very thick.

68. *TOMATO/RICOTTA DRESSING*

Yield: 5 cups

The list of ingredients looks pretty long, I dare say, but really they are things that you mostly have to hand anyway. You virtually chuck them into the blender or food processor in the order given and, hey presto, you have a scrummy dressing, dip or sandwich spread.

½ bunch parsley (75-100 g) — roughly chopped
a few celery tops (25 g) — roughly chopped
400 g tomatoes — roughly chopped
½ teaspoon sea salt
1 tablespoon dehydrated tomato flakes

500 g fresh ricotta cheese
1 teaspoon sweet red paprika
3 tablespoons lemon juice
1 tablespoon Herbed Apple Cider Vinegar (recipe 146)
2 tablespoons cold pressed vegetable oil

Finger Food Meals

Finger food meals should be served much more often. Kids love them. I think they like the freedom of being allowed to use their fingers, but also they like eating their vegetables raw and in largish chunks or pieces and, of course, the vegetables are very recognisable — also important to kids. However, it's not just kids that like finger foods; the cook should like them a lot because of not having to do so much preparation (although it is important to take enough time to present the foods attractively) and adults in general seem to enjoy the more casual atmosphere of such a meal.

The three main ingredients of a finger food meal are: (i) vegetables and fruit; (ii) breads or crackers; (iii) cheeses and/or dips. If you want a 'slap up' meal, put out a board with lots of fancy cheeses and several dips plus a few different sorts of breads and crackers. However, for a simple family meal, one or two cheeses and/or dips will suffice, with one sort of bread and lots of fruit and vegetables.

Vegetables to consider are: beans, broccoli flowerets, carrot sticks, cauliflower flowerets, celery sticks, Chinese cabbage leaves, cucumber, lettuce leaves, peppers, baby mushrooms, snow peas, spring onions, tomatoes, zucchini sticks — all raw, of course.

Following are recipes for some dips and a pâté which you can make with a blender or food processor. However, if you don't possess one you can still prepare them with the help of a potato masher and/or sieve.

69. VEGETARIAN PÂTÉ

Yield: 1½ cups

I don't think it is possible to achieve that liver flavour from non-meat products. However, this pâté has the correct consistency and the flavours are good enough to make it a worthwhile contribution to your board.

½ cup fine buckwheat noodles
25 g butter (see Butter versus
  Margarine)
2 cloves garlic
2 tablespoons port
1 tablespoon dried sage
1 dessertspoon salt-reduced soy
  sauce (available at health food
  shops or Asian groceries)

3 tablespoons brose meal (pea
  flour)
75 g tofu (buy it where you buy
  your soy sauce)
a couple of grindings of black
  pepper and allspice (see
  Cooking Notes)
another 25 g butter

Boil the buckwheat noodles in salted water until soft (about 5 minutes). Drain and place in the food processor with the first 25 g butter and the remaining ingredients. Process until smooth and then pour the mixture into a small earthenware terrine. Bake in a moderate oven (180°C/350°F) for 50 minutes with the lid on.

Finally, remove the lid, place the second 25 g butter on top and cook for a further 10 minutes.

Serve cold in the terrine, garnished with parsley sprigs.

70. HUMMUS

Yield: 2 cups (if thinned with about ½ cup liquid)

This dip is usually made with tahini, sesame seed paste. However, I've found that kids don't like its taste at first. Certainly, if yours do like tahini, add some to the recipe, as sesame seeds are very nutritious

2 cups cooked chickpeas (about
  150 g dried)
3 tablespoons lemon juice
2-3 cloves garlic
pinch sea salt

Garnish:
olive oil
red paprika
parsley — finely chopped

Blend or mash all ingredients together until a smooth cream results. Add a little of the cooking liquid as necessary.

Spread the paste on a flat plate, make a little indentation in the middle and fill this with olive oil. Now sprinkle sweet red paprika around the edge of the oil and garnish the centre with chopped parsley. As people dip in their Middle Eastern bread, they will mix the garnishes into the paste.

PEANUT PROTEIN DIP

71.

Yield: 1½ cups

This is a firm dip and, if desired, it could be quite easily moulded into a shape between the hands and coated in sesame seeds.

150 g tofu
3 rounded tablespoons unsalted
  peanut butter
1 teaspoon soy sauce

2 tablespoons cold pressed
  vegetable oil
1 tablespoon sesame seeds

Process all ingredients except for the sesame seeds. Press the mixture into a serving bowl and top with sesame seeds and a bright garnish (stuffed olive slices, for example).

TOMATO TOFU DIP

72.

Yield: 1½ cups

This dip makes a good dressing, too. It will thicken a little on standing.

1 medium tomato
1 spring onion
100 g tofu
2 tablespoons cold pressed
  vegetable oil

3 rounded teaspoons Honey
  Mustard (recipe 139)
1 pinch kelp powder
1 pinch marjoram
1 pinch oregano

Process all ingredients until fairly smooth.

CURRY DIP

73.

Yield: 1 generous cup

1 cup well-cooked leftover red
  lentils
1 scant teaspoon curry powder

1 clove garlic
1 tablespoon homemade fruit
  sauce or chutney (see recipes
  143-5)

Process all ingredients until fairly smooth.

74. *HERBED POTATO DIP*

Yield: 1½ cups

This is a firm dip. If you would like a runnier one, add up to another ⅛ cup of water.

300 g well-cooked leftover	*1 teaspoon dried sage*
potatoes	*1 pinch vegetable salt*
25 g parsley	*⅛ cup cold pressed vegetable oil*
1 clove garlic	*⅛ cup water*
1 pinch marjoram	*2 teaspoons kelp granules*

Process all ingredients, except for the kelp, until smooth. Finally, mix the kelp granules through.

This looks wonderful if served with tomatoes and black olives.

75. *SWEET AND PINK DIP*

Commence preparation in advance
Yield: 1¾ cups

This dip is better the next day when the gherkin flavour has permeated all.

100 g well-cooked beetroot	*⅛ cup cold pressed vegetable oil*
(unseasoned)	*50 g Gherkins (recipe 140)*
250 g well-cooked potato	

Process all ingredients together.

76. *PINK PEAR DIP*

Yield: 1½ cups

1 very ripe or even overripe pear	*1 heaped teaspoon sweet red*
1 cup creamed cottage cheese	*paprika*
	1 heaped teaspoon Honey
	Mustard (recipe 139)

Process all ingredients until smooth. Use the same day and don't try to store overnight.

GHERKIN DIP   77.
Yield: 1½ cups

150 g cottage cheese
100 g Asian tofu (see Cooking
    Notes)

50 g home-made Gherkins
    (recipe 140)
⅛ cup liquid from the gherkins

Process all ingredients until smooth.

DEEP SEA DIP   78.
Yield: 3¼ cups

When I was pregnant last year I started getting cravings for prawns. As I
have a personal commitment not to eat anything that has been a living
'critter', I decided that it might be possible to allay the craving with
seaweed, as I probably just needed iodine or something that both seaweed
and shellfish have in common. I therefore devised this dip which tastes a bit
like a prawn dip.

50 g 'Mekabu' seaweed
    (available at your health food
    store)
300 g cream cheese or creamed
    cottage cheese
1 teaspoon honey
½ teaspoon sea salt
2 tablespoons dehydrated
    tomato flakes

3 tablespoons lemon juice
1 tablespoon Worcestershire
    sauce (Newman's brand
    contains no dead animal and
    the least offensive list of
    ingredients.)
1 teaspoon sweet red paprika

Soak the seaweed for 10-20 minutes and steam it until soft; then blend or
puree it. Beat it together with all the other ingredients.

Soups

In my experience children don't like most soups. This may have something to do with their inbuilt knowledge of what is good for them — a knowledge which they bring with them into the world but which often gets distorted by an intake of chocolate and other strongly flavoured drugs which are sweet to taste. Most soups have the guts cooked out of them and, in addition, the food swimming in all the liquid is not good as it dilutes the digestive juices. Raw soups, like gazpacho for instance, which are basically pulverised vegetables are quite different, of course. However, they usually have too strong a flavour for children, plus the fact that the ingredients are all mixed up and unrecognisable turns kids off.

However, I have included a few soups which, from my experience, kids do like, just because there are times when soup and hot bread for lunch is very tasty, warm, filling and even a weekend treat. I use soup sometimes for no other reason than that it saves us making complete pigs of ourselves with the bread straight from the oven.

Another reason I have for making soup is to use up the vegetable stock in the freezer. Whenever I steam vegetables or dried beans I pour the liquid into a container in the freezer. As a result, when I come to make soup I have an iceblock with different striations representing the various meals cooked — 1 cm of beetroot water, 2 cm of bean water, 1 cm of potato water, etc.

If you use a container with sloping sides and no ridge around the neck, you can easily remove the stock iceblock if you happen to have forgotten to take it out of the freezer in time or if you have to make an impromptu meal. Just sit the container in hot water for a couple of minutes and the stock will slip out easily.

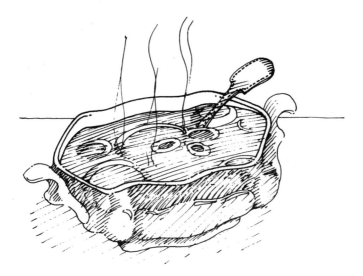

IDENTIFIABLE TOMATO AND VEGETABLE SOUP

Serves 8

79.

Yes, it sure is a peculiar name! But I wanted to remind you of what I said in the introduction, that kids like readily identifiable food — not concoctions. You will see that I use dehydrated tomato flakes. I use these for two reasons — in winter they are more economical and more flavoursome than the real thing, and they are probably just as good for you as cooked tomatoes, as they don't contain preservatives or additives. Of course, when tomatoes are plentiful, I wouldn't consider anything else.

3 cloves garlic — crushed or
  very finely chopped
1 tablespoon dried basil
1 tablespoon oil
1½ litres vegetable stock (or
  water is satisfactory)
3 tablespoons dehydrated
  tomato flakes (or 4-5 tomatoes
  if plentiful)

125 g wholemeal noodles
4 medium-sized potatoes —
  chopped into small dice
450 g French beans — cut into
  lengths of 2-3 cm
150 g Australian gouda cheese
  — grated

Saute garlic and basil in the oil. Add stock, tomato flakes, noodles and potatoes. Bring to boil, turn back and simmer. Five minutes later add the beans.

When just cooked, serve with some grated cheese on top.

80. MYSTERY VEGETABLE SOUP
Serves 8

Having just finished saying how kids like to have their vegetables readily identifiable, here I am with a mystery soup. Just what is she on about? ! ! My first statement still stands — but there are times when a mother just has to get rid of something in the refrigerator or garden which little junior doesn't like, especially of the green leafy variety. It's for the purpose of camouflaging these unloved vegetables that this soup has been devised. Basically, the aim is to mask unwanted flavours with other stronger flavours which are liked.

1 large onion — finely chopped
2 teaspoons dried basil
1 tablespoon oil
1½ litres vegetable stock (or water)
125 g wholemeal noodles
3 tablespoons dehydrated tomato flakes

600 g mixed vegetables to be used up, e.g. broccoli stalks and leaves, zucchini, spinach stalks and leaves, chokoes, etc.
1 medium carrot
a little chopped parsley
a few chopped black olives
a little grated cheese (fetta is good) if a real camouflage job is necessary.

Saute onions and basil in the oil. Add stock, bring to the boil and add noodles and tomato flakes.

While they are cooking chop very finely the vegetables to be camouflaged, preferably in a blender or food processor using the metal blade. Slice or chop the carrot so that the pieces still look like carrot (assuming junior likes carrot).

Now add the processed vegetables and carrot to the simmering noodles which should be just about cooked. Simmer for a short while — so that the green vegetables retain a little brightness and the carrot pieces a little crispness.

Serve with chopped parsley (this also helps to camouflage the green 'mystery' vegetables), olive pieces and/or grated cheese.

81. PUMPKIN SOUP
Serves 8

Yuk! pumpkin. Yes, I feel the same. However, as long as the pumpkin is balanced by the bland potato, the result is more than pleasing.

200 g onion — finely chopped   *1 litre stock and/or water*

75 g butter (see Butter versus
  Margarine)
a couple of grinds of black
  pepper, preferably mixed with
  allspice (see Cooking Notes)

900 g potato — cut in large dice
800 g butternut pumpkin —
  roughly chopped

Saute the onion in the butter. Grind in spices. When the onion is soft add the stock, potato and pumpkin and cook until the potato is soft.

Then put the soup through the food processor, blender, food mill or sieve until a smooth consistency is achieved.

Serve with a dob of cream or yoghurt and nutmeg sprinkled over it.

POTATO SOUP
82.
Serves 4

This soup uses up those ends of asparagus which are too tough to serve. If you wish to give the soup an asparagus flavour, you will have to double the quantity used. As it is, the recipe is intended for kids who don't like asparagus, but whose parents want them to eat it anyway.

The way to prepare the asparagus is as follows. After purchase (or cutting from the garden) bend the asparagus spear so that it snaps in the middle. The top half is just nice for steaming, and may be put aside for that purpose as it's not needed for this recipe. Now take a sharp knife and, starting from the snapped end of the bottom half, cut off little circles of asparagus (about ½ cm long) and continue cutting until the knife meets too much resistance. At this point even lengthy cooking of such a tiny piece will result in a stringy product and you can stop cutting. Interestingly, these little pieces of asparagus are quite acceptable raw in a salad. Somehow, they then feel crisp only and not stringy.

1 large brown onion — finely
  chopped
40 g butter (see Butter versus
  Margarine)
600 g potato — cut into large
  dice
ends (cut as above) of 18 fat
  asparagus spears (or 300 g)
500 ml stock and/or water

black pepper, preferably mixed
  with allspice (see Cooking
  Notes)
4 heaped tablespoons finely
  chopped parsley (It is essential
  to have about one heaped
  tablespoon of parsley per
  serving as the flavour of the
  soup is otherwise too bland.)

Saute onion in the butter until soft. Add vegetables, stock and a grinding of black pepper and allspice.

After the vegetables are cooked, blend or sieve and serve with the parsley stirred in at the last moment.

83. PEA AND TOFU SOUP

Commence preparation in advance
  Serves 6

In this soup the tofu is treated so that it somewhat resembles ham. Normally I do not subscribe to the use of 'pretend' meat. However, this is such a tasty way to serve tofu that I think it is well worth it. The tofu is not added to the soup until the last minute, as it quickly loses its crunchiness in the soup.

1½ cups split peas
2 tablespoons oil
1 large onion — finely sliced
1 clove garlic — crushed
2 teaspoons ground cumin seed
1 teaspoon turmeric
2 cups of diced vegetables
  (Tomatoes are really nice; so
  perhaps use 1 cup of them and
  1 of broccoli or silver beet
  stalks — anything which
  needs using up.)
1 litre vegetable stock

Tofu sippets:
1 more clove of garlic —crushed
2-3 tablespoons oil
250 g tofu — sliced (about ½ cm
  thick postage stamp-sized
  pieces)
soy sauce

Soak the split peas in water, preferably overnight, and then simmer until they are broken up. Now saute in oil the onion, the first clove of garlic and the spices and then add the other vegetables and continue cooking until just tender. Then combine the vegetables and spices with the split peas and add the stock.

Meanwhile, saute the second clove of garlic in oil and add the tofu to the pan when the garlic is soft. When the tofu pieces are crisp and brown, liberally spinkle them with soy sauce.

Add the tofu sippets to the soup and serve immediately.

Breads and Pastries

PASTRY *84.*
Yield: see para. 1

This recipe makes sufficient for at least two 24 cm diameter pastry bases or, if rolled thinly between plastic, two bases and two tops.

Pastry is always a bit tricky with wholemeal flour, but, by rolling it between sheets of lunch wrap or plastic, a good result can be obtained. See also Cooking Notes.

3 cups plain wholemeal flour
(see Cooking Notes)
3 teaspoons baking powder

100 g butter (see Butter versus
Margarine)
1-1¼ cups water

If you use the larger amount of water, the pastry becomes so wet that it will have to be pressed into the pie plate. However, the result is a scrummy 'cakey' pastry. (Note, though, that all flours vary in their water holding capacity.)

In the food processor, with the metal blade in place, mix the flour and baking powder. Then add the butter in a few big chunks and process by 'pulsing' for a second or two at a time — on and off — until the butter seems to be evenly distributed. Then add water and process until the dough is well mixed.

If making your pastry by hand, sift the flour and baking powder together (chuck the bran left in the sifter back into the mixture) and either cut the butter in with two knives or rub it in with your fingers until the mixture looks like coarse breadcrumbs. Then add the water a little at a time, mixing it to a smooth dough.

85. NON-WHEATEN PASTRY

Yield: one 23 cm top and bottom

This pastry actually handles better than many wholemeal wheaten pastries. See also Cooking Notes.

½ cup wholemeal rye flour
½ cup stone ground buckwheat flour
¾ cup stone ground barley flour

¼ cup polenta (corn meal)
2 teaspoons baking powder
70 g butter (see Butter versus Margarine)
⅔ cup water

Sieve together or mix well the flours and baking powder. Rub the butter in until the mixture resembles coarse breadcrumbs. Mix the water in and form the dough into a soft ball.

86. ALMOND SHORT CRUST

Yield: 30 cm (12 inch) flan

A delicious crust for dessert purposes. Actually this makes a bit more than enough for a 30 cm flan and you can add more honey to any leftover dough and bake it as cookies.

1 dessertspoon honey
about ¼ cup warm water
185 g almonds — crushed finely (freshly done)
185 g plain wholewheat (or rye) flour (see Cooking Notes)

6 rounded dessertspoons soy flour
¼ teaspoon ground cloves
½ teaspoon ground cinnamon
250 g butter (see Butter versus Margarine) at room temperature

Stir the honey into the warm water to dissolve and leave it until cool before using in the dough.

Combine the freshly crushed or ground almonds with the flours and spices. Rub in the butter using the method you usually follow for making pastry — between the fingers, with two knives or pulsing in the food processor.

When the mixture resembles coarse breadcrumbs, add the honey and water to form a smooth dough. Press it into the flan dish with your floured fingers and/or a spatula as it is too sticky to roll.

Bake in a moderate oven (180°C/350°F) for 15-20 minutes.

RAINBOW CHAPATIS
Yield: 17 chapatis

87.

I have called these rainbow chapatis as, while each one is one colour only, it is possible to make several different colours — marvellous for a 'chapati party'. The colours are achieved by using different vegetable purees: beetroot, broccoli, carrot, pumpkin, silver beet, tomato, or even zucchini and chopped herbs for a spotted result. The vegetable puree should be made simply of steamed vegetables pureed without liquid if possible — otherwise use the tiniest amount only. Beetroot, though, is too firm to puree without liquid, and, in addition, needs a little oil mixed in with the flour or else it won't hold together well. Tomato needs no cooking, of course.

This is a beaut recipe for feeding the kids spinach or pumpkin or any other unloved vegetable, as the flavours are not strong at all. Even the fussiest eaters like these chapatis, especially if you don't reveal what's in them till after they've 'proved the pudding'. A word of warning: the green vegetable puree is pretty 'urky' and, when mixed with the flour into dough, looks positively revolting — Emma says like squashed slugs and snails. However, once it's cooked it looks fine and tastes magnificent spread with cream cheese and sandwiched together with salad vegetables.

If you fry the chapatis in salted butter (see Butter versus Margarine), they won't need any more salt; otherwise they may need a little salt added.

1 cup vegetable puree   *1½ cups plain wholemeal flour*

Mix together, adding more flour if necessary. Pinch off pieces and roll between the palms of the hands into walnut-sized balls; then sit them on a floured board. Now roll them flat and fry in a heavy pan at a pretty high temperature. As they start to bubble, turn and do the other side.

If you suffer from a wheat allergy, you could use the following mixture of flours. However, you will have to roll the chapatis a bit thicker and take a little more time and care in cooking them as they are not as flexible as wheaten ones.

½ cup stone ground millet meal   *½ cup wholemeal rye flour*
½ cup stone ground buckwheat   *2 tablespoons soy flour*
*   flour*   *1 cup vegetable puree*

88. *COCONUT BREAD*
Yield: 20 cakes

So simple and quick to make, this tasty bread — a bit like chapatis — is great to whip up and serve with finger foods or soup for unexpected guests.

If cooked in salted butter (see Butter versus Margarine), there is no need to salt the dough; otherwise a pinch or two will do for this tiny amount.

*4 tablespoons dessicated
coconut
6 tablespoons plain wholewheat
(or rye) flour*

pinch cayenne pepper

Mix all the ingredients together and add cold water to form a soft dough. Pinch off small pieces and roll into little flat cakes, thicker than chapatis — about ½ cm thick and 4 cm diameter. Fry them until golden brown.

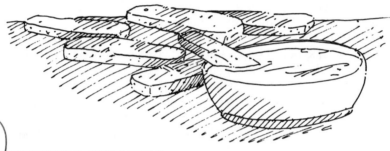

89. *CHEESE STICKS*
Yield: 50-80 cheese sticks

An old favourite which is just as good with wholemeal flour; and the kids love them in their lunch boxes or for parties.

*250 g plain wholemeal flour
(rye can be substituted)
¼ teaspoon curry powder
(optional)
1 teaspoon baking powder*

*½ teaspoon sea salt
100 g butter
150 g cheese — grated
½ cup water (approximately)*

Make up the dough, following your usual method. Mix the cheese through after rubbing in the butter. Then mix in enough water to make a stiff dough, roll it out on a floured board and cut it into sticks or any desired shape.

Bake on unoiled baking sheets in a moderately hot oven (190°C/375°F) for 20 minutes.

CHEESE AND HERB LOAF 90.

Yield: 1 loaf tin

1 cup wholemeal rye flour
½ cup stone ground barley flour
¼ cup stone ground millet meal
¼ cup stone ground buckwheat
  flour
1 teaspoon bicarbonate of soda

1 tablespoon dried sage or dried
  mixed herbs
150 g tasty cheese — grated (1¼
  to 1½ cups)
1 cup milk

Sieve together or mix well the dry ingredients, mix the cheese in and finally the milk.

This mixture is very stiff and looks as though it could be kneaded — just like a yeast bread — but *don't* try it, as the result is tough and awful.

Bake in a buttered and papered loaf tin at 180°C/350°F for 50 minutes.

CUMIN LOAF 91.

Yield: 1 loaf tin

If you don't like the strong, earthy flavour of cumin seeds, use carraway. They're both delicious, although your kids might object if not used to them.

1 cup wholemeal rye flour
½ cup stone ground barley flour
¼ cup brown rice flour
¼ cup stone ground millet meal
3 teaspoons baking powder

1 tablespoon partly ground
  cumin seeds
½ teaspoon sea salt
1 cup water
¼ cup oil

Sieve together or mix well the dry ingredients and then add the water, mixing until a very soft dough is formed.

Bake in a well buttered (see Butter versus Margarine) and papered loaf tin at 180°C/350°F for 35-45 minutes.

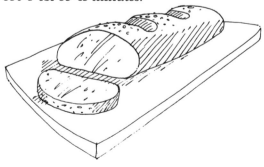

Desserts

WHY NOT TRY DESSERT-ONLY MEALS?

If you're a bit hung up on ensuring you feed the family enough protein, desserts can be a great help. Personally, I'm hung up on not having too much sweet tack in the diet and not forcing down the first course to get to the dessert, and that's why dessert-only meals really appeal to me. We usually have a dessert-only meal at the weekend — occasionally during the week — and I always serve it with extra fruit, mostly raw.

You'll see that when sweetener is called for I always use honey in my recipes. Maple syrup is good, too, but pure maple syrup is too expensive for most of us to consider, and there's no point buying imitation maple syrup. Most people know that sugar (even so-called 'raw' sugar) is useless as a food. However, very few yet realise that it actually has a very bad effect on the body in that it is so 'refined', i.e. has so much taken out of it, that it draws minerals out of the body when being digested. Honey, on the other hand, is a complete food. Some people say to me, 'But my dentist says that honey is the worst thing for teeth,' and I reply to them that of course sticky honey on bread or, even worse, on a dummy, is bad for the teeth — so would sugar-based stickjaw toffee be. However, when honey is used as a sweetener in puddings, etc., it is no worse for the teeth than sugar. That's not to say that it is exactly good for them, but we've all had our palates spoiled to some degree, haven't we?

PANCAKES — EGGLESS

92.

Yield: 15 saucer-sized pancakes

This is a great treat which the kids can make all by themselves and therefore get more pleasure out of it. (Mothers get lots of pleasure by having a rest, too!) Serve with raw grated apples or pears, cinnamon, natural sultanas and pure cream or coconut cream.

If wheat is an allergen for you, you can make these using brown rice and wholemeal rye flours half and half. However, rice/rye pancakes should be cooked slowly but surely, as they don't hold together as well as wheaten ones.

*2 cups plain wholemeal flour
(see Cooking Notes)
2 rounded dessertspoons soy
flour*

*2 rounded dessertspoons millet
flakes
3 cups water*

Mix well, adding the water a little at a time, or blend all the above ingredients and then pour into a lipped jug.

Heat a heavy skillet or frying pan and fry the pancakes in melted butter (see Butter versus Margarine). Before pouring each batch, give the mixture a stir in the jug as it settles.

Just a word about the millet flakes — apart from being very good for you, they are necessary as a sort of aggregate in your slurry to hold it together. If you don't have millet flakes (although I suggest you buy some) don't just leave them out, substitute bran or something similar.

93. PINEAPPLE/COCONUT CHEESECAKE

Serves 6-8

Crust:
100 g butter
50 g plain whole wheat (or rye)
  flour
50 g honey
100 g dessicated coconut
50 g sesame seeds

Garnish:
½ cup dried pineapple pieces
  —sliced

Filling:
1 good cup Pineapple Butter
  (recipe 138)
600 g cream cheese
1 tablespoon honey
1 x 250 ml container of
  unsweetened coconut and
  pineapple juice
4 teaspoons agar powder (see
  Cooking Notes)

Crust:
Melt the butter in a medium-sized saucepan and cook the flour for a couple of minutes while you are getting out the other ingredients and weighing them. Take the saucepan off the heat and put it on your scales (with something under the pan so that the scales don't melt, if they're plastic). Now weigh the honey directly into the saucepan so that you don't have any sticky spoons or cups to clean — but be careful, as 50 g of honey is really only one big blob. When the honey has dissolved, quickly mix in the remaining crust ingredients and then press the mixture into a 19 cm (7 in.) spring form pan (cake tin with removable base). Refrigerate until the filling is made.

Filling:
Beat together the Pineapple Butter, cream cheese and honey and set aside. Tip the coconut and pineapple juice into a large saucepan and stir in the agar. Bring almost to the boil and simmer for 2 or 3 minutes. Now take the cream cheese mixture and combine it with the agar mixture, in stages, stirring to ensure that the agar does not set in a hard lump. Agar sets when lukewarm and therefore it has a tendency to set when the cold cream cheese hits it. By stirring it in stages you can ensure that it remains above the setting temperature until the whole of the mixture is incorporated.

  Fill the prepared crust, garnish with the pineapple and refrigerate until needed.

APPLE AND ALMOND CHEESECAKE   94.

Serves 6-8

Crust:
100 g butter
100 g plain whole wheat (or rye)
  flour
70 g honey
100 g almonds — ground

Garnish:
A few slivered almonds

Filling:
2 Granny Smith apples —sliced
  thickly and lightly steamed
550 g cream cheese
3 teaspoons pure almond
  essence
4 tablespoons apple juice
  concentrate (or 3 tablespoons
  honey)
1 teaspoon agar powder (see
  Cooking Notes)
½ cup water (or apple juice)

Crust:
Melt the butter in a medium-sized saucepan and cook the flour for a couple of minutes, stirring all the while. Take the saucepan off the heat and put it on your scales (with something under the pan so that the scales don't melt, if they're plastic). Now weigh the honey directly into the saucepan so that you don't have any sticky utensils to clean. When the honey has dissolved, quickly mix in the ground almonds and then press the mixture into a 19 cm (7 in.) spring form pan (cake tin with removable base).

Filling:
Lay the steamed apple slices over the bottom of the crust and refrigerate.
  Beat well or blend the cream cheese and flavourings and set aside.
  Dissolve the agar in the liquid in the bottom of a large saucepan and simmer for a couple of minutes, stirring occasionally.
  Pour the cream cheese mixture into the agar in stages, stirring constantly so that the agar does not set. (It sets at room temperature.) When all the cream cheese has been incorporated and the agar evenly mixed through, pour it into the prepared base, garnish and refrigerate.

95. NON-DAIRY YOGHURT PIE

Serves 6-8

Sesame seeds in the crust give added calcium to compensate somewhat for the lack of milk products.

Crust:
100 g butter (or, if you're really strict about the non-dairy business, you could use ¼ - ⅓ cup oil — but it's not as good, see Butter versus Margarine)
50 g plain whole wheat (or rye) flour
50 g honey
50 g sesame seeds
50 g wheat germ or bran or a mixture of both
50 g rolled oats

Filling:
zest of 1 lemon — finely chopped (can be omitted if you double the vanilla)
50 g honey
50 g lecithin granules
250 g tofu
1 cup plain soy yoghurt
⅓ cup cold pressed vegetable oil
2 teaspoons pure vanilla essence
¼ cup water
4 tablespoons lemon juice
2 teaspoons agar powder (or 2 rounded tablespoons agar flakes) (see Cooking Notes)

Crust:
Melt the butter in a medium-sized saucepan and cook the flour for a couple of minutes while you are getting out the other ingredients and weighing them. Take the saucepan off the heat and put it on your scales (with something under the pan so that the scales don't melt, if they're plastic). Now weigh the honey directly into the saucepan so that you don't have any sticky spoons or cups to clean — but be careful, as 50 g of honey is really only one big blob. When the honey has dissolved, quickly mix in the remaining crust ingredients and then press the mixture into a 19 cm (7 in.) spring form pan (cake tin with removable base).

Filling:
Mix well or blend all ingredients, with the exception of the agar, water and lemon juice. Beat until it begins to froth and set aside.

Put the water and juice in a small saucepan, stir in the agar and bring almost to the boil. Then simmer for a couple of minutes until the agar has dissolved. The agar should then be dribbled into the filling mixture while you are agitating it or added a little at a time if you are mixing by hand.

Pour the completed mixture into the prepared crust and refrigerate. Top with fresh fruit (strawberries or Chinese gooseberries are best, I think).

You can turn this into a very animal thing, by using cottage cheese instead of tofu and milk yoghurt instead of soy. If you replace soy yoghurt with milk yoghurt, you'll probably need only half the quantity of lemon as it is more tangy.

FRUIT CRUMBLE 96.

Really, every time I make a fruit crumble it can turn out differently. So I won't give exact amounts or ingredients, but simply list the different things you can use. As long as you have a fruit layer below a crumble layer, you have a fruit crumble!

Fruit layer:
Sliced and cored apple or pear, whole bananas, sliced pineapple, whole berries, apricot halves, thick slices of peaches.

Leave the fruit raw as it will have quite enough goodness cooked out of it by the time the top is browned, although apples can be lightly steamed first.

Sprinkle some cinnamon and/or mixed spice over the fruit, if you like.

Crumble layer:
There are three basic needs: fat, sweetener and dry 'crumbles'. For the fat you can choose either butter or cold pressed vegetable oil, enough to moisten the dry goodies. For the sweetener use honey (easy to use if heated with the butter and then mixed into the dry ingredients), or just put lots of dried fruit pieces in with the crumble. As far as the dry goodies are concerned, the list is almost unending, but it's usual to start with plain wholewheat or rye flour (stone ground, organically grown, of course) and then add about twice as much crunchy stuff, e.g. shredded coconut, rolled oats, rolled wheat, sesame seeds, sunflower seeds, nuts, peanuts, lecithin, hulled millet, buckwheat, bran, etc.

When you have mixed the crumble layer put it on top of the fruit layer and bake in a moderate oven (180°C/350°F) until the top is crunchy and the bottom soft.

Just in case you're still uncertain how to proceed, the other day when I made a crumble I took note of what I put in and here it is. Incidentally, I used much more than my recommended twice as much crunchy stuff as flour. So you see that it is such a casual affair that it really doesn't matter what you use.

Serves 8-10
Fruit layer:
1¼ kg fruit

Crumble layer:

½ cup oil and butter (see Butter versus Margarine) mixed
¼ cup honey
½ cup plain wholemeal or rye flour

1¼ cups rolled oats
⅜ cup sesame seeds
½ cup nuts
¼ cup lecithin granules
¼ cup rice bran

97. JO'S PEACHES
Serves 8

On the night of our 18th wedding anniversary, our friend Jo was staying with us, and she and our girls, Emma and Mia, decided to give us an impromptu slap-up dinner to celebrate.

That night also happened to be the eve of our baby Peter's birth (two weeks late) and I hadn't kept up with the marketing too well. When it came to making a dessert, we had only the remains of a case of peaches, nine dried figs and some dried pineapple. The result was terrific:

9 dried figs (1 generous cup when chopped)
150 g dried pineapple pieces (1 generous cup when chopped)

¾ cup flagon port (½ + ¼)
¼ cup water
12 freestone yellow peaches — halved and stoned

Chop the figs and pineapple and cook for 5 minutes in ½ cup port over a low heat to soften slightly. Stir occasionally.

Mix the final ¼ cup of port with ¼ cup of water and pour into the base of an earthenware baking dish.

Arrange the peach halves, cut side up, in the baking dish and spoon the softened fruit into the tops of the peaches.

Cook for 20-30 minutes in a moderately low oven (160°C/325°F).

CARAMEL BANANAS
Serves 4

98.

This is a very rich and filling dessert which, if it follows another course at all, should be preceded by something light.

3 + 1 ripe bananas
⅓ cup pitted dates
25 g butter (see Butter versus Margarine)
1 dessertspoon honey
3 dessertspoons Soy Compound (from your health food shop)

¼ + ¼ cup water
1 cup millet flakes
¼ cup sesame seeds
⅔ cup shredded coconut
¼ cup pecan nuts for garnish

In a generously buttered ovenproof dish arrange three of the bananas, split lengthwise — split side up.

Now blend the remaining banana with the dates, butter, honey, Soy Compound and the first quarter cup of water until fairly smooth. (If doing this step by hand you must chop the dates finely and heat all until soft before mashing well.) Spoon two good tablespoons of this mixture over the bananas in the dish.

Now add the second quarter cup of water and the cereals and coconut to the mixture remaining and blend or mix again. Spoon this mixture over the bananas. The first mixture, being runny, drips down between the bananas like a sauce, whereas this dryer mixture forms a topping.

Finally, slice the pecans lengthwise, each into three or four pieces, and scatter them over the top. Bake in a moderate oven (180°C/350°F) for 15-20 minutes.

99. VANILLA CUSTARD
Serves 6-8

This custard is very well liked by kids — it seems that only the real 'custard haters' won't even give it a go. Whenever I think of this custard I remember the time when I was camp cook for Mia's class at the beach. I had planned a lunch of yoghurt, fruit salad, shredded coconut, nuts and vanilla custard as a change from sandwich-type lunches, and had catered accordingly. However, the teacher planned to go to a neighbouring beach for the day. Undaunted, I cooked the custard after breakfast and got my lunch-rostered helpers to make the fruit salad and pack up the other ingredients. We told the children to take along a bowl and spoon (and a cup for juice, of course). When lunchtime arrived we spread all the ingredients out on a little tablecloth on the sand and half a dozen adults presided over them. The children queued along the beach and got a dollop of this and a dollop of that, according to their requests. About two (out of thirty) did not want the custard — which was lukewarm now, as it was in a heavy saucepan and had been left in the sun to keep warm — and more than half wanted seconds, but, unfortunately, there were none.

100 g butter (see Butter versus Margarine)
75 g brown rice flour and 50 g maize flour (semolina can be substituted if you like)

5 cups milk (or soy milk)
¾ cup honey
2-3 teaspoons pure vanilla essence

Melt the butter and stir in the flours. Keep stirring for a couple of minutes and then add the milk, honey and vanilla. Stir with a wooden spoon until thickened.

This custard is also nice made with rosewater instead of vanilla, and I think it is cheaper, too.

PEARS IN PORT 100.

Most people have eaten pears in red wine which contains piles of sugar, but if you use port you get only natural grape sugar. The only drawback with port is that it does not yield so much syrup when boiled down.

Choose nicely shaped pears with their stems intact, peel them and stand them up in an ovenproof dish. Sprinkle them liberally with cinnamon and then cover (if possible) with a mixture of port and water, either 2 to 1 or 1 to 1. If it's not possible to cover them, you will have to turn them all over halfway through the cooking process.

It is possible to cook them on top of the stove, but I think the oven gives a better result, especially if you are using an earthenware baking dish. I prefer to start cooking them a few days before they are needed. I put them in a moderately slow oven for about an hour; thereafter I put them in the oven every time I use it. In this way, the pears get a long thorough baking and they become almost like jam and extremely difficult to handle as they are so soft. However, they are absolutely delicious. They probably have no nutritive value left, but it's nice to splurge occasionally! By the way, they shrink when cooked, so you can overload the dish to start with.

TOFA 101.

Tofa, a type of bean curd similar to tofu, is sold in larger Asian groceries. It has a consistency a little like smooth junket but is much nicer. It is served by the Chinese as a dessert with sugar and water syrup. Try it with pure maple syrup — yum!

FRESH FRUIT TART 102.

How attractive is a platter of fresh fruit after dinner, but if you want to serve something a little more fussy, you can arrange your fruit in a tart.

Use Almond Short Crust (recipe 86) and bake it blind (without the filling in it). When it is cool, arrange prepared fruit on it. The fruit can be any or some of: apricot halves, berries, peach slices, pineapple pieces, Chinese gooseberries, grapes, mandarins, stoned cherries.

Take a little apple juice and add agar powder or flakes to it (powder in the proportion 1 teaspoon to 1 cup liquid, and flakes in the proportion 1 tablespoon to 1 cup liquid). Bring it almost to the boil and simmer for 2 or 3 minutes, stirring until the agar dissolves. Pour the liquid over the prepared flan and put it aside to set.

Iced Desserts

Some of these 'icecreams' have only the natural sweetening from dried fruit. This is quite sufficient. However, you may wish to add honey at first, and, when you have your family 'hooked' on the recipe, gradually cut down the honey until you can at last remove it altogether. I did this with my family and now, if I know we are having sweet-toothed visitors, I make the ices with honey and my family complains that they are too sweet!

By the way, I have used the term 'icecream' very liberally. Iced treat or iced confection might be better names — not only do they not contain cream, but most contain no animal protein at all.

Most home-made icecream needs to be frozen in a churn, but these are okay without. As they freeze very hard, leave plenty of time before serving them to allow them to soften. If they do thaw completely they can simply be re-frozen.

Having said all this, I would suggest you first try the icecreams before you freeze them as they make nice 'creams' to have with fruit. I believe freezing should be avoided where possible. Also, these creams make ideal infant food.

103. PIPPY ICECREAM
Serves 4-6

This is not only good for the kids; the adults appreciate its tangy taste.

1 cup raw cashew pieces	*⅓ cup water*
⅓ cup cold pressed vegetable oil	*1 tablespoon honey*
2 very ripe bananas	*2 Chinese gooseberries (Kiwi*
1 very heaped tablespoon soy	*fruit)*
milk powder	*5 juicy passion fruit*

Finely crush the cashew pieces in a blender or food processor and then add oil and bananas and continue blending until a smooth mixture results. Next add all remaining ingredients except gooseberries and the passion fruit pulp which should be blended for a few moments only after the icecream base is smooth and creamy. Freeze in the ice compartment of the refrigerator.

If you don't have a blender or food processor, I think you shouldn't even attempt this one, as the cashews have to be ground into very fine meal and it is too tedious to do this by hand.

RED BERRY ICECREAM
104.

Serves 4-6

*100 ml unsweetened raspberry
and apple juice concentrate
(from your health food shop)
4 ripe bananas*

*4 tablespoons milk powder
½ cup cold pressed vegetable oil
1 cup strawberries*

Blend or mash together all ingredients except the strawberries, which should be chopped and stirred through just before freezing.

RAIDERS
105.

Serves 8

Why the name? Two reasons — to my mind the ingredients conjure up the land of the pyramids, and the lucky eaters of this treat will be so healthy and have so much energy that they too can perform marvellous feats with a whip!

*2 cups well cooked brown rice
½ cup cold pressed vegetable oil
100 g pitted dates
50 g dried figs*

*2 very large (or 4 small)
bananas
juice of 2 oranges
1 cup milk powder (or soy milk
powder)
100 g natural sun-dried sultanas*

Pulverise the rice with the oil in the blender or food processor until quite smooth. (If you have to do this by hand, it would be better to buy brown rice flour instead of rice and cook it up with water into a porridge or custard.)

Roughly chop up the dates, figs and bananas and juice the oranges. Add them to the rice with the milk powder and blend until smooth again. (To do this by hand, cook the finely chopped dried fruit in the orange juice to soften it and then mash in the bananas before adding to the rice and milk powder.)

Finally, fold in the sultanas and freeze.

106. APRICOT ICECREAM

Serves 4-6

This icecream is free of animal protein.

150 g dried apricots
¾ cup water
1 teaspoon agar powder (see
   Cooking Notes)

350 g Asian tofu (see Cooking
   Notes)
½ cup cold pressed vegetable oil
3 tablespoons Soy Compound
   (from the health food shop)

Chop the apricots roughly and bring to the boil in the water. Simmer for 3-4 minutes and then leave to soak until the fruit is well swollen.

Drain the fruit and reserve any liquid. Make the liquid up to ¼ cup with more water and stir in the agar. Set this aside for the moment.

Now blend all the other ingredients together until smooth (or mash very well).

Simmer the water and agar for 2-3 minutes and then add it to the icecream while it is still being agitated to avoid the possibility of jelly lumps forming when the hot agar meets the cool icecream. (To do this by hand, agitate the mixture with one hand while you pour in the water and agar with the other.)

Freeze in the ice compartment of the refrigerator, but do remember to try it first, as you may change your mind and serve it unfrozen.

If you like, you may omit the agar. The resulting frozen product is less smooth and has less protein and minerals but is still quite satisfactory.

CARROT AND WHATCHASAY? 107.

Serves 8-10

This is a great icecream to make if you have a particularly troublesome eater, because of the vegetables it hides.

1 teaspoon agar powder (see Cooking Notes)
150 ml water
1 heaped tablespoon honey
3 cups raw cashew pieces
1 apple — washed with skin left on
100 g celery stick
50 g mung bean shoots
1 cup soy milk powder

250 g carrots — juiced (Orange juice can be substituted, in which case you need 175 ml, but try to get hold of a juicer and use the carrot juice as it's much better.)
1¼ cups natural sun-dried sultanas (Sulphured sultanas are not nearly so good in icecream and, of course, not nearly so good for the body. But, goodness aside, you haven't lived until you've tasted a frozen natural sultana!)

Dissolve the agar in the water, add the honey and set aside.

Pulverise the cashew pieces in the blender or food processor until quite finely ground. Next add the apple, celery and bean shoots and blend until a smooth paste results. Add the soy milk powder and carrot juice and blend again until quite smooth.

Now simmer the honey, agar and water for 2-3 minutes and then add it to the icecream while it is being agitated, to avoid jelly lumps.

Finally, fold in the sultanas and freeze.

(If you don't have a blender or food processor, forget this one, as it is too tedious to grind the cashews into fine meal by hand.)

108. PINEAPPLE ICECREAM

Commence preparation in advance
Serves 4-6

Another very simple yet effective icecream.

200 g dried pineapple pieces	*350 g Asian tofu (see Cooking*
¾ cup water	*Notes)*
1 teaspoon agar powder (see	*⅓ cup cold pressed vegetable oil*
Cooking Notes)	

Bring the pineapple pieces and water to the boil, simmer for 3-4 minutes and leave to stand until the fruit is well swollen, preferably overnight.

Drain the fruit and reserve any liquid. Make the liquid up to ¼ cup with more water and stir in the agar. Set this aside for the moment.

Now blend all the other ingredients until smooth (or mash well).

Simmer the water and agar for 2-3 minutes and then add it to the icecream while it is still being agitated, to avoid any lumps.

Freeze in the ice compartment of the refrigerator.

To make this recipe even simpler you may omit the agar. The resulting product will have less protein and minerals and won't be so creamy, but it is quite satisfactory.

109. LEMON ICECREAM

Really, this must be the simplest of recipes, and you can no doubt think of other combinations.

leftover Vanilla Custard (recipe	*Eggless Lemon Butter*
99)	*(recipe 137)*

Simply blend equal quantities together until smooth, then freeze in the ice compartment of the refrigerator.

If you want to keep some custard for this recipe, I suggest you use my trick of taking it out of the pot and hiding it in the refrigerator before the meal. Otherwise, the family will find the pot after dinner and lick it clean.

NUTAPPLE ICECREAM 110.

Serves 4-6

1 cup hazelnuts
4 very ripe bananas
½ cup milk

¼ cup natural unsweetened
  apple juice concentrate
¼ cup cold pressed vegetable oil

Grind the hazelnuts into a fine meal, mash the bananas well and beat all ingredients together until smooth. Then freeze in the ice compartment of the refrigerator.

This is another recipe that is too laborious to make without a blender or food processor.

INDIA TREAT 111.

This sweet treat is very reminiscent of many Indian desserts flavoured with rosewater. If your children like Turkish delight, they will probably like this too, although, of course, the textures, etc., are very different.

It is more like an iceblock; so freeze it in iceblock trays.

200 g dried lima beans
½ 25 ml bottle rosewater
1 tablespoon beetroot juice

1 250 ml pack coconut juice
3 dessertspoons honey

Soak, cook and drain the lima beans. Pulverise in the blender or food processor until smooth and add the remaining ingredients (the beetroot juice for colour). Freeze.

(If making this by hand, ensure that the lima beans are well and truly cooked and mash them vigorously as you need to get a nice smooth paste for icecream. Fortunately, lima beans do break up easily.)

CARROT CURDIE 112.

Serves 4-6 as a drink

This is another recipe which is very handy for children who are real problem eaters. It is nice as a drink and kids find it delicious as iceblocks.

300 g Asian tofu (see Cooking
  Notes)
2 tablespoons cold pressed
  vegetable oil
2 heaped tablespoons honey

2½ cups freshly made carrot
  juice
1 cup soy milk powder
2 teaspoons pure vanilla extract

Blend or mash all ingredients together and chill or freeze as desired.

Cakes, Cookies
& Party Treats

113. SPICE CAKE

This cake is light yet moist and the consumer won't guess that it contains *NO EGGS* and *NO SUGAR*, or even honey. What's more, the dates can't even be detected. This cake does tend to dry out fairly quickly so don't keep it for more than a day or so.

175 g chopped dates	*2 teaspoons bicarbonate of soda*
250 ml milk	*3 teaspoons mixed spice*
225 g wholemeal flour	*100 g butter*

Place the dates and milk together in a saucepan, simmer for 10 minutes and leave to cool for 20 minutes or so. It must not be so hot that it melts the butter in the next phase. Blend or beat until smooth

If you are using a food processor it is simpler to leave this wet beating stage until after the dry dough stage described in the next paragraph. Then remove the dry dough and use the processor work bowl for the date 'mush', and then mix the two together.

Meanwhile, proceed with the dry ingredients as though you are making pastry. Mix the flour, soda and spice well. Rub the butter in until the mixture resembles coarse breadcrumbs. Or, if using a food processor, switch the motor on and off quickly until the same result has been achieved.

Butter and paper a loaf tin (see Cooking Notes) and pre-heat your oven to 180°C/350°F.

Now mix the date 'mush' in with the dough. The result will be a rather firm mixture which should then be transferred to a buttered and papered loaf tin.

Bake for 1-1¼ hours in a moderate oven (180°C/350°F).

Ice with Milky Frosting (recipe 122) and sprinkle fruit medley (chopped dried fruit mix) over that.

KIDS' OWN FRUIT CAKE 114.

Most kids object to fruit cake because of the mixed peel. This one has dehydrated pineapple in it instead, and it sure is popular.

Make the whole Spice Cake (recipe 113) and fold in at the end:

100 g dehydrated pineapple pieces — roughly chopped
25 g dried apricots — roughly chopped

50 g natural sultanas
50 g currants
25 g walnut pieces
25 g almonds — roughly chopped

Because of the extra bulk of the fruit and nuts, the yield is nearly doubled, so that you could use two loaf tins.

CARROT AND PINEAPPLE CAKE 115.

150 g dehydrated pineapple pieces — roughly chopped
1½ cups grated carrot
¼ cup water

225 g wholemeal flour
2 teaspoons bicarbonate of soda
4 teaspoons cinnamon
100 g butter (see Butter versus Margarine)

Simmer the pineapple pieces, carrot and water in a saucepan for 5 minutes and leave to cool for 20 minutes or so. It must not be so hot that it melts the butter in the next phase.

Next butter and paper a loaf tin (see Cooking Notes) and pre-heat your oven to 180°C/350°F.

Mix or process the flour, bicarb. and cinnamon together well and rub in the butter as though you were making pastry.

Mix or beat the pineapple and carrot mixture in with the dough.

Put in a buttered and papered loaf tin and bake for 1-1¼ hours in a moderate oven (180°C/350°F).

Delicious with Milky Frosting (recipe 122).

116. LEMON CAKE

Another very simple cake, based on pastry making methods. Unfortunately, though, it tends to be dry by the second day.

> *225 g wholemeal flour*
> *2 teaspoons bicarbonate of soda*
> *100 g butter (see Butter versus*
> *Margarine)*
>
> *½ cup honey*
> *1 cup Eggless Lemon Butter*
> *(recipe 137)*

Rub or process the butter into the flour and bicarb. by whatever means you prefer. Then beat the honey and Lemon Butter in, and that's that!

Put in a buttered and papered loaf tin and bake in a moderate oven (180°C/350°F) for 1-1¼ hours.

Yummy with Milky Frosting (recipe 122).

117. BANANA AND CAROB UPSIDE DOWN CAKE

As with most of these cakes based on the pastry making principle and made with wheat flour, this one tends to dry out quickly and therefore shouldn't be kept for too long. That won't represent a problem, however, as it will be gobbled up very quickly. As the ingredients are all good and there is not too much sweetening, you needn't be worried for your family's health.

> *150 g chopped dates*
> *200 ml milk*
> *225 g wholemeal flour*
> *2½ teaspoons bicarbonate of*
> *soda*
> *4 tablespoons carob powder*
>
> *100 g butter + a little more (say*
> *10 g) for dotting the top*
> *(bottom)*
> *3 small bananas + more for*
> *decorating the top (bottom)*
> *1 scant dessertspoon honey*

Simmer the dates and milk together for 10 minutes. Cool for 20 minutes.

Meanwhile, mix the flour, bicarb. and carob very well and rub in or process the 100 g butter as if you were making pastry.

If you are using a food processor it is simpler to leave the wet beating stage until after the dry dough stage. Then remove the dry dough and use the processor work bowl for the date 'mush', and then mix the two together.

Mash well or blend the date and milk mixture with the three bananas.

To prepare your loaf tin, butter and paper it fully. Then slice more bananas into ½ cm slices and arrange on the bottom, remembering that the bottom will become the top when the loaf is inverted after cooking. Now drizzle a scant dessertspoon of honey over the banana slices and dot with a little butter. Pre-heat the oven to 180°C/350°F.

Beat the dough and the date mixture together and pour into the loaf tin, covering the sliced banana. Bake for 45 minutes at 180°C/350°F.

When the cake is done, run a knife around the edges to ensure it is loose and tug at the paper lining so that the cake comes out. Sit it, upside down, on a rack to cool. Remove the paper carefully so that the banana pieces don't stick to the paper. A sharp knife blade held between the paper and the bananas will help.

BARLEY BANANA CAKE 118.

Another good recipe for people with wheat and milk allergies. Naturally you would have to substitute margarine for the butter, although I do not subscribe to the use of unnatural things (see Butter versus Margarine). (Psst! Why not try to get hold of some unpasteurised cream and make your own butter? You would probably find that you weren't allergic to it, because the enzymes are still alive and kicking in raw milk.)

225 g chopped dates	100 g stone ground buckwheat
400 ml water	flour
2 small bananas	4 teaspoons ground cinnamon
300 g stone ground barley flour	3 teaspoons sodium bicarbonate
50 g stone ground millet meal	150 g butter

Butter and paper a 20 cm (8 in.) diameter tin.

Bring the dates and water to the boil, simmer for a couple of minutes and leave to cool so that the mix does not melt the butter in the next step. Mash the bananas and cooled date and water mix together.

If you are using a food processor it is simpler to leave this wet beating stage until after the dry dough stage described in the next paragraph. Then remove the dry dough and use the processor work bowl for the date 'mush', and then mix the two together.

Sieve together or mix well the flours, spice and bicarb. Rub or process the butter into the flours until the mix resembles coarse breadcrumbs.

Mix the date and banana mush into the flours and beat well.

Bake at 180°C/350°F for 50-60 minutes.

119. RYE, RUM AND RAISIN SLICE

This is a strongly flavoured slice which would be more economical if you reversed the rum to water ratio. However, I would urge you to try it this strong way. If you can tolerate milk powder, make Milky Frosting (recipe 122), add carob powder to it and ice the slice for a rich effect.

Butter and paper a tin about 20 x 26 cm (8 x 10 in.).

100 g chopped dates	*1 teaspoon sodium bicarbonate*
½ cup rum	*1 teaspoon cinnamon*
¼ cup water	*50 g butter (see Butter versus*
120 g wholemeal rye flour	*Margarine)*
	150 g raisins

Bring the dates, rum and water to the boil. Simmer for a couple of minutes and then leave to cool so that the mix does not melt the butter in the next stage. If the dates have not mushed up properly in the rum, break them up with the back of a spoon.

If you are using a food processor it is simpler to leave this wet beating stage until after the dry dough stage described in the next paragraph. Then remove the dry dough and use the processor work bowl for the date 'mush', and then mix the two together.

Sieve together or mix well the flour, bicarb. and cinnamon. Then cut or process the butter in the flour as though making pastry. When the flour resembles coarse breadcrumbs, mix in the date mush and beat well. Finally, fold in the raisins.

Bake at 180°C/350°F for 20-25 minutes.

120. HONEY AND ALMOND LOAF

This loaf has a good flavour, albeit a little 'thin' tasting because of the lack of milk or fat. So, if you don't have to watch what you eat, use milk instead of water. You can even fortify it with additional milk or soy milk powder for extra richness.

1 cup wholemeal rye flour	*4 tablespoons honey*
½ cup stone ground millet meal	*3 teaspoons pure almond*
½ cup brown rice flour	*essence*
1 teaspoon sodium bicarbonate	*12 almonds — sliced into three*
1¼ cups water	*or four pieces each*

Mix well or sieve together the flours and bicarb. Heat the water in a small saucepan and dunk the first tablespoon of honey in it. The honey will leave the spoon readily when the water is hot enough and then the subsequent tablespoons are very easy to measure and to clean off. When the honey is stirred in, add the almond essence and then mix or process the liquid into the mixed flours. Beat well.

Pour the resultant runny mixture into a well buttered (see Butter versus Margarine) and papered loaf tin. (Because there is no fat in this loaf it will even stick to the paper unless it is quite oily.) Sprinkle the sliced almonds on top.

Bake at 180°C/350°F for 50 minutes.

BARLEY AND APPLE CAKE　121.

'So he put the barley cakes his mother had baked for him into his pocket, and his axe over his shoulder, and set off for the dark forest. By noon he was hungry and sat down on a large smooth rock to eat one of his cakes when a strange little man dressed in grey approached from nowhere and asked if he could have some of his barley cake. The boy rudely told him to go away as he could not spare any for him.'

How many fairy stories begin like this? Anyway, whenever I pack barley cake for Emma and Mia for lunch I remind them to share their cake with whoever might ask, just in case an awful spell is cast upon them too.

½ cup water	*100 g butter (see Butter versus*
½ cup honey (about 175 g)	*Margarine)*
175 g stone ground barley flour	*½ average Granny Smith apple*
50 g wholemeal rye flour	*— grated*
1½ teaspoons baking powder	*½ average Granny Smith apple*
2 teaspoons cinnamon	*— sliced — for decoration*

Heat the water and dissolve the honey in it. Set aside to cool a little. It must not be so hot as to melt the butter in the next stage.

Mix well or sieve together the flours, baking powder and cinnamon. Chop or process the butter into the flours as though making pastry, stopping when the mix resembles coarse breadcrumbs. Add the liquid and beat well. Fold in the grated apple and transfer the mixture to a buttered and papered loaf tin. Decorate the top with apple slices and sprinkle with a little more cinnamon if desired.

Bake at 180°C/350°F for 55-60 minutes.

122. *MILKY FROSTING*

Yield: If your measure is a teaspoon, enough to ice 1 cake.

22 parts milk powder
4 parts water

2 parts oil
3 parts honey

Whip or beat the milk powder and water together and, while still agitating, drizzle in the oil and honey. The mixture stiffens more on standing. Alternatively, mix the wet ingredients well and then beat in the milk powder.

Use as is or flavour with essence or spice.

If you would like carob frosting, substitute 4 parts of carob powder for the same quantity of milk powder and omit 1 part honey, as carob is naturally sweet.

123. *PEANUT COOKIES*

Yield: 24 cookies

Oh so peanutty! They are also very sweet; so you might prefer to use just two tablespoons of honey and, in that case, 1 tablespoon of water.

100 g + 100 g unsalted peanuts
100 g butter (see Butter versus
Margarine) at room
temperature

3 tablespoons honey
100 g plain whole wheat (or rye)
flour

Grind 100 g of the peanuts and put the second 100 g aside.

Beat the butter and honey with the ground peanuts. Add the flour and beat again, and finally fold in the second 100 g peanuts.

Drop the mixture from a dessertspoon onto a baking sheet (which does not need to be oiled), leaving about 3 cm space between each to allow for a little spreading. Bake at 160°C/325°F for 20 minutes.

This is another recipe that is too laborious to make without a blender or food processor.

ALMOND BISCUITS 124.

Yield: 40 small biscuits

The kids love these and yet they're fine enough for afternoon tea with the silver service.

100 g almonds
100 g butter (see Butter versus Margarine) at room temperature

3 tablespoons honey
50 g plain whole wheat (or rye) flour

Grind the almonds, add the butter in pieces and the honey and beat well. Finally mix in the flour. Drop the mixture from two teaspoons onto baking sheets (which do not need to be oiled), leaving a fair bit of space to allow for spreading in cooking. Bake at 160°C/325°F for 15 minutes.

This is another recipe that is very tedious to make without a blender or food processor.

SESAME COOKIES 125.

Yield: 20 cookies

Good for everyone, but especially for allergy sufferers.

100 g sesame seeds
100 g butter (see Butter versus Margarine)
3 tablespoons honey

50 g brown rice flour
25 g wholemeal rye flour

Cream together the seeds, butter and honey and then mix in the flours. Spoon from two dessertspoons onto baking sheets (which do not need to be oiled). Leave 2 to 3 cm between each cookie to allow for a little spreading. Bake at 160°C/325°F for 20 minutes. Allow the cookies to cool a little before removing from the tray.

126. MULTI-GRAIN SULTANA COOKIES

Yield: 40 cookies

100 g butter (see Butter versus
Margarine)
2 tablespoons honey
25 g millet flakes (rolled millet)
25 g bran-germ (omit if wheat is
an allergen and then double
millet flakes)

5 tablespoons milk or water or
grape juice
25 g rice bran
25 g buckwheat flour
100 g rolled oats
100 g natural sultanas

Beat together the butter, honey, flakes and bran-germ. Then add the liquid.
Mix in the rice bran, flour and oats and finally fold in the sultanas.
    Drop from a teaspoon onto a greased tray. They don't spread.
    Bake at 160°C/325°F for 15-20 minutes.

127. MUNCHY CRUNCHY HOBBIT GOBBLES

Yield: 24 patty pans

At birthday parties, these are always first to go. The beauty of them is that
the kids can actually make them themselves.

60 butter (see Butter versus
Margarine)
3 tablespoons honey
4 cups unsweetened puffed
wheat (or rice)

2 tablespoons Soy Compound
(from your health food shop)
up to 90 g peanuts (optional)

Melt the butter and honey together. Meanwhile, mix the dry ingredients in
a large bowl. When the butter and honey are melted, pour them over the dry
ingredients and mix quickly, coating all the puffs.
    With dessertspoons, fill paper patty pans and bake in a moderately low
oven (160°C/325°F) for 5-10 minutes.
    Unsweetened puffed rice (from the health food shop) can be substituted
for the wheat if wheat is an allergen, but I think the wheat is a bit nicer.

TOFFEE NUTS

128.

Yield: 20 patty pans

These can be a bit deadly for the teeth if cooked for the whole time, when they really are like toffee. You may prefer to cut the cooking time down, as every minute makes for a more brittle product.

200 g honey	*200 g almonds*
100 g butter (see Butter versus	*50 g shredded coconut*
Margarine)	*100 g barley flakes*

Put a large saucepan on the scales and weigh the honey directly into it. Now place it on the heat with the butter and, after they have melted and dissolved and mixed together, allow them to bubble for another 6-7 minutes on a low heat. Stir often or the mixture will catch.

Mix the dry ingredients in quickly. Then spoon into paper patty pans and allow to cool and harden.

AUSSIE CHRISTMAS

129.

Yield: 55 postage stamp-sized pieces

This is a healthy, slightly suntanned version of White Christmas.

½ cup honey	*1 cup almonds — crushed to a*
200 g creamed coconut	*coarse meal*
1 cup water	*⅓ cup natural sultanas*
1 cup unsweetened puffed	*⅓ cup chopped dried apricot*
wheat (or rice)	*⅓ cup chopped dried pineapple*
½ cup milk powder	*1 cup dessicated coconut*
½ cup Soy Compound	
(from your health food shop)	

In the top of a double saucepan melt the honey and creamed coconut with the water.

Mix the remaining ingredients well and, when the honey and coconut mixture is melted, pour it in and mix all together quickly.

Spread onto a plastic plate, mark into squares and refrigerate. Cut when cold. Keep in the refrigerator.

130. DELICIOSITY

Yield: 45 postage stamp-sized pieces

This is nice for kids' parties, but adults really go for it in a big way as an after-dinner treat.

1 cup rolled oats	½ cup chopped walnuts
125 g butter	3 tablespoons Soy Compound
3 tablespoons honey	(from your health food shop)
1 cup chopped dates	2 teaspoons pure vanilla essence
1 cup chopped dried apricots	3 tablespoons carob powder

Process the oats until they resemble wheatgerm or bran in size. Then add the butter and honey and continue processing until smooth. The remaining ingredients can be added a little at a time while the processor is still going.

The resulting fairly homogenous, brown tacky paste should be spread onto a plastic plate and refrigerated. When cold it can be cut into shapes and removed from the plate quite easily.

(If you don't have a blender or food processor, you could use half a cup of bran instead of the rolled oats and cook the remaining ingredients until they're soft enough to mash.)

131. TROPICAL TREATS

Yield: 30-36 large cherry-sized balls

Another success with the young and old alike.

100 g raw cashew nuts	50 g creamed coconut
100 g dried pineapple pieces	shredded coconut for coating
1 small very ripe banana	balls

Pulverise the cashews in the food processor. Tear the pineapple pieces into three or four pieces each as you put them into the processor with the banana. Chop the creamed coconut into the processor and blend until the heat melts the coconut pieces.

Roll the mixture into balls in shredded coconut. Refrigerate for longer life.

(If you have to make these by hand, crush the cashews with a rolling pin, or even under Granny's flat iron, mince the pineapple, mash the banana, melt the creamed coconut in the top of a double saucepan, and then mix them all together well.)

APRICOT GOODNESS BALLS 132.

Yield: 24 balls

I could subtitle these 'calcium balls', but then they are also rich in potassium and iron.

100 g dried apricots — chopped	*1 teaspoon pure orange essence*
100 g dried figs — chopped	*6 tablespoons sesame seeds for*
1 cup well cooked red lentils	*coating balls*
2 tablespoons honey	*12 Brazil nuts (optional)*
2 tablespoons milk powder	

Process all ingredients together, except for the sesame seeds and Brazil nuts. Roll the mixture into balls in the sesame seeds.

For a final touch if liked (and for even more calcium), take a dozen Brazil nuts, cut them in halves and poke a half into each ball. Refrigerate for longer life.

(To make by hand, mince the dried fruits, mash the lentils and mix well with the remaining ingredients.)

LEMON AND APRICOT SLICE 133.

Yield: 25 pieces

1 cup rolled oats	*50 g dried apricots — chopped*
60 g cream cheese	*50 g dessicated coconut*
½ cup Eggless Lemon Butter	*40 g hazelnuts for decoration*
(recipe 137)	

Process or blend all ingredients, except the hazelnuts, together. Alternatively, beat all the ingredients together well after passing the apricots through a food mill.

Spread the paste onto a plastic plate and refrigerate. Cut into shapes when cool. Place a hazelnut in the middle of each shape.

134. CAROB MINT SLICE

Yield: 30 postage stamp-sized pieces

½ cup boiling water
2 to 3 tablespoons dried
   spearmint leaves
1 cup barley flakes (rolled
   barley)
4 tablespoons milk powder

2 tablespoons carob powder
50 g dates — chopped
2 tablespoons honey
50 g dessicated coconut
50 g walnuts — chopped
50 g natural sultanas (optional)

Make a very strong cup of mint tea with the water and spearmint leaves, cover and leave to steep for at least 15 minutes.

Process the barley flakes until they resemble bran in size and then add the milk powder and carob powder. Next add the chopped dates, honey and coconut and the complete cup of mint tea (leaves and all). Process well. Finally fold in the walnuts, and sultanas if used.

Spread onto a plastic plate and refrigerate until firm when the slab can when the slab can be cut into squares or diamonds, etc.

(If making this without the aid of a food processor, use ½ cup bran flakes instead of the barley, although the final texture may not be as nice. Heat the honey and dates with the mint tea and mash well. Mix all ingredients well.)

135. NATURALLY NICE NIBBLES

Yield: 5 cups

A good savoury party treat or lunch box snack.

⅓ cup oil
1 rounded teaspoon prepared
   curry powder
3 cups puffed wheat (or 2 cups
   and 1 cup home made
   popcorn)

½ cup peanuts
½ cup almonds
½ cup raw cashews
½ cup natural sultanas

Heat the oil in a large heavy skillet and fry the curry powder for a couple of minutes. (If your kids like spicy foods, you could add cumin seeds and/or garlic at this stage also.) Throw in the grains and nuts and fry, stirring all the while. Just before the ingredients appear done, stir in the sultanas.

Serve cold (if you can stop it being eaten for that long) and store any leftovers in an airtight container.

Quick and Easy Bottles and Preserves

FRUIT BUTTERS

Fruit butters are somewhat old-fashioned but are all set to make a comeback, as they don't require sugar. In addition, with the modern equipment available to us, there is no need for tedious sieving of the cooked fruit, which was probably the reason that fruit butters went out of style originally.

Jams, being full of sugar, keep a long long while. However, fruit butters keep only a matter of weeks, and even then I prefer to keep mine in the refrigerator as I'm not a very efficient steriliser of jars and lids. So make up only a couple of kilos of fruit at a time. Actually, this makes it less of an ordeal and therefore more easily faced than a whole day's jam making.

It's probably safer to sterilise your jars by placing them in a cool oven (120°C/250°F) for 15 minutes, but I don't bother, as our fruit butters never hang around long enough to go off. They seem to keep in the refrigerator for three weeks.

Wash, slice and core or stone the fruit. Skins may be left on if clean. Cook gently until tender with just sufficient water to prevent burning. Process the cooked fruit and return it to the pan. Simmer gently until it begins to sputter, add cinnamon and cook until it passes the test. The test is to place a little fruit on a plate and leave it to cool. If the liquid does not separate out, it is done. Fill sterilised (or very clean) jars with the fruit butter and seal.

Apples make the best fruit butters, either alone or with other fruit such as pears or dried vine fruits or even fresh grapes. Actually, you can experiment with anything in plentiful supply, even tomatoes, which might be nice with, say, cheese as a sandwich filling.

137. EGGLESS LEMON BUTTER
Yield: 5 x 500 g jars

This economical recipe fills five 500 g jars with enough left over to have a good on-the-spot tasting.

1 kg pumpkin
500 g honey

500 g butter (see Butter versus
Margarine)
4 large juicy lemons

Cook the pumpkin and mash well.

Sit the saucepan on top of the scales and pour your honey straight in so that you don't have sticky utensils. Alternatively, buy a 500 g jar of honey and use the lot!

Add the butter and cooked pumpkin to the saucepan and start them heating slowly while preparing the lemons.

Wash the lemons and cut into eighths, remove pips and pulverise in the food processor. (If your lemons are very pithy, the result will be too bitter for most kids' palates. In that case, either cut off most of the pith before processing or else use the juice and zest only. If you choose the latter, your yield will be reduced.) Add the lemon pulp to the contents of the pan, bring slowly to the boil and then simmer with the lid off for thirty minutes, stirring occasionally. If there are still tiny lumps of lemon peel and you want a completely smooth puree, blend the lemon butter again before bottling. Refrigerate when cool.

(A word of warning — this recipe always 'blomps' when cooking, even when turned very low; so don't stand near the pot with your best clothes on.)

PINEAPPLE BUTTER 138.
Yield: 4 x 500 g jars

This butter is worth having on hand for school lunches, as it is a sweet treat
without too much honey.

800 g pumpkin flesh
600 g sweet pineapple flesh
(from 1 small pineapple. You
can even use the core if you
have a food processssor or
blender.)

300 g honey
400 g butter

Steam the pumpkin in as little water as possible.

If using a blender or processor, blend the cooked pumpkin and the raw
pineapple.

Put a large saucepan on the kitchen scales and weigh the honey straight
in to avoid mess and waste. Add the butter and the fruit pulp and cook by
simmering very gently for 1¼-1½ hours. Stir occasionally — more often after
the first hour. Cool and put in jars. Refrigerate.

(If making by hand, cook the pineapple and the pumpkin with the
butter and honey and press all through a sieve towards the end of the
cooking time when the fruit is soft enough.)

HONEY MUSTARD 139.

This is a recipe which cannot be made in the food processor or by hand
— even though our not too distant forebears probably made it by hand
with a mortar and pestle. It needs the strong pulverising action of the
blender to grind the mustard seeds easily.

250 g yellow mustard seeds
250 g brown mustard seeds

2¼-2½ cups apple cider vinegar,
depending on how fine the
seeds are ground
1½ cups honey (more if your
taste requires it)

Grind the seeds in the blender in three or four batches. Now blend in all the
remaining ingredients and bottle in dry jars sterilised in a 120°C/250°F
oven for 15 minutes.

140. GHERKINS

Yield: About 1 kg gherkins

Like sauce and pickles, gherkins are something we should not eat too much of, but they are wonderful for using in dips and sandwich spreads, and maybe even to camouflage a failed main course.

Old-fashioned gherkin recipes tell you to pack the fruit in salt for a couple of days or soak it in brine, but this results in an extremely salty product. The reasons for this treatment are two, as far as I can gather. One is that salt is a natural preservative and tends to kill off any bugs hanging around the gherkin skins; the second is that salt draws out some of the gherkin liquid and therefore allows for more ready penetration of the pickling liquid. There are ways around this. If you want complete penetration of the vinegar in a short time, slice the fruit. If you feel the need to kill off the bugs and don't think the vinegar will do so, either pack the gherkins in salt overnight only (and give them a good wash next morning to remove the salt — and maybe add new bugs?!) or par boil them. I personally think that a thorough wash and quick pickling in sterilised jars is sufficient. To sterilise the jars, place them in a 120°C/250°F oven for 15 minutes.

The method is simply to put the prepared fruit in the jars and cover with pickling vinegar, which is made as follows:

1 litre apple cider vinegar   *25 g cloves*
25 g blade mace (optional)   *25 g cinnamon stick*
25 g allspice   *6 peppercorns*

Tie the spices in a muslin bag and dunk into the pan of vinegar. Bring slowly to the boil, simmer for a few minutes with the lid on and then remove from the heat and allow to stand for a couple of hours. After removal of the spice bag, the vinegar is ready for immediate use or can be stored for later.

This recipe is sufficient to pickle about 1 kg of gherkins, depending on their size and of course the size of the jars. If the gherkins are sliced they will pack down much more economically.

GINGER HONEYED PICKLES   141.

Pickles are really easy to make and, while I don't use them very often as vinegar is a bit of a no-no, they are very handy as a basis for dip and they also are good used sparingly in stir-fried vegetables.

2 kg mixed vegetables
100 g ginger root (or more if the
flavour of ginger is really
appreciated)
salt (if required)
500 ml apple cider vinegar

500 ml water
6 peppercorns
6 whole allspice
10 mustard seeds
2 cups honey

Slice the vegetables so that they will look good in the jars. For instance, button mushrooms can be left whole, fat carrots can be sliced across, cauliflowers cut into flowerets, peppers into rings, turnips into dice, etc. If you wish to salt the vegetables, spread them out in a large earthenware or glass dish and salt between layers. Leave for twenty-four hours and then rinse and drain the vegetables. However, before doing this read my note on salting preserves under Gherkins (recipe 140).

Heat the other ingredients together until the honey dissolves. Pack sterilised jars with the vegetables and top up with the pickling liquid. Sterilise jars in a 120°C/250°F oven for 15 minutes.

If your lids are metal, line them with paper or the vinegar will corrode them.

ORANGE HONEYED PICKLES   142.

This recipe makes a really delicious pickle for a spread or dip.

1 kg mixed vegetables
zest of 1 orange
salt (if required)
250 ml apple cider vinegar
250 ml water
6 peppercorns

6 whole allspice
¼ teaspoon ground cloves
3 sticks cinnamon — broken
into 2-3 cm pieces
1 cup honey
juice of 1 orange

Follow the method for Ginger Honeyed Pickles (recipe 141).

143. APPLE SAUCE

2½ kg apples
1 kg onions
3 teaspoons ground allspice
4 teaspoons ground cloves

500 g honey
1¼ litres apple cider vinegar
pinch of cayenne

Wash, core and chop the apples and put them in the food processor with the metal blade in place. Similarly process the onions. Put the resulting pulp with the other ingredients in a saucepan and simmer all till it is a good colour and consistency, about 1-1½ hours.

Sterilise bottles in a 120°C/250°F oven for 15 minutes before putting the hot sauce in them and sealing.

(If you don't have a processor, you'll have to pass the mixture through a sieve when cooked.)

144. PLUM SAUCE

Plum sauce is probably the most flavourful of all home-bottled sauces. It is certainly the cheapest for most people, as nearly everyone knows someone who has a plum tree that drops plums unwanted and unloved all over the footpath. The only problem is that it is such a nuisance to have to sieve the cooked fruit to remove all the stones. Actually, it is surprising how little they weigh; so you can use this recipe for both large and small plums. If you need to thin it more, simply add a little more vinegar before removing the finished sauce from the heat.

3 kg plums
750 g honey
750 ml apple cider vinegar
1 teaspoon sweet red paprika

1 scant teaspoon cayenne
 pepper
1 tablespoon cloves
25 g root ginger — bruised

Simmer all ingredients for 1½-2 hours in a saucepan and then strain through a sieve. Bottle immediately in warm sterilised bottles and seal using paper under the lid to avoid corrosion. Sterilise the bottles in a 120°C/250°F oven for 15 minutes.

145. TOMATO SAUCE

Once again the food processor turns an arduous task into a simple one.

2 kg red tomatoes
150 g honey
250 ml apple cider vinegar
pinch cayenne pepper
1 rounded teaspoon sweet red
 paprika

1 rounded teaspoon ground
 allspice
1 rounded teaspoon ground
 cloves
1 rounded teaspoon ground
 cinnamon

Wash and roughly chop the tomatoes and then process them until pulverised. Put the tomato pulp and the remaining ingredients into a large pan and simmer, stirring from time to time until the sauce is smooth. Bottle immediately in warm sterilised bottles and seal using paper under the lid. Sterilise bottles by placing in a 120°C/250°F oven for 15 minutes.

(Again, if you don't have a food processor, sieve the mixture when cooked.)

HERBED APPLE CIDER VINEGAR 146.

Any vinegar can be herbed, but I use only apple cider vinegar as it is reputedly 'better for you'. Indeed, there is a whole branch of folk medicine which recommends apple cider vinegar and honey for clearing out many ills from the body. From the culinary point of view, ordinary vinegar seems much sharper on the palate — another reason for using apple cider vinegar.

The taste of herbed vinegar is so much superior to the plain product, the herbing task is as easy as falling off a log, and an added bonus is that the bottles look pretty on a shelf in the kitchen. They give a warm country kitchen glow to the room — and for so little effort, too. So please give it a go.

Almost any fresh herbs can be used. Tarragon and thyme are the prettiest in the bottle. At times fruit shops sell bunches of herbs and they are almost always available at markets. If you buy your herbs, you will want to put up a few bottles at once to use them up; otherwise do a bottle or two at a time from your own garden supply. I have even been known to scrounge around looking for things to put in my vinegar and have picked wild fennel tops from around the creek, added celery tops, a clove of garlic and a few dried seeds (cardamom, cumin, etc.) — and voilà, a tasty vinegar in a few week's time after maturity.

Choose attractive bottles if possible, wash them thoroughly, almost fill them with apple cider vinegar, and then poke the herbs in as you will. Experiment with different combinations or else keep them simple — it's up to you. A clove of garlic never goes astray and maybe a few whole allspice or other seeds. Put a piece of paper inside the lid to hinder corrosion and a circle of material over the outside to look pretty. Arrange the bottles on the shelf to look attractive and await the moment when you can give your cooking that extra zip. When the greens have lost their brightness and gone olive coloured you will know that moment has arrived. The vinegar will keep almost indefinitely, and, when it is finished, use the herbs blended with cottage cheese as a dip or spread.

Breakfasts

147. AUTUMN MUESLI

 Fruit-wise, autumn is always sad for me as it means the passing of the luscious summer fruits for yet another year. This muesli captures some of the late summer/early autumn fruits and might be worthwhile making in a larger quantity to put aside for the winter months. (I would refrigerate it if storing it for that long just in case any little moist pockets remain after toasting.)

Another advantage offered by this recipe is the very small quantity of oil and honey needed.

1 fresh fig — stalk cut off, no need to peel	*1 cup shredded coconut*
1 very ripe pear — cored	*1 cup millet flakes*
½ very ripe banana	*1 cup rolled barley*
½ cup grapes — seeded	*½ cup rice bran*
⅔ cup oil	*½ cup mixed chopped nuts*
⅓ cup honey	*1 cup raw peanuts*
	5 cups rolled oats

Mash well or blend the fruit and place in a medium-sized saucepan. Pour the oil into your cup measure and then the honey; so, if you get it out again quickly and into the saucepan with the pureed fruit, the honey won't stick to the measure. Place the saucepan over a low heat and allow the mixture to bubble.

Mix the dried ingredients well in a large bowl and pour the bubbling fruit mixture over them, stirring quickly so that each little flake is coated.

Spread the mixture into two large baking dishes and bake in a low oven (140°C/300°F) for about 1 hour. Stir often.

GENEVIEVE'S MUESLI 148.

My friend Genevieve makes the most delicious muesli I've ever tasted.

½ cup oil
½ cup peanut butter
¾ cup honey
4½ cups rolled oats
1 cup millet flakes

½ cup milk powder (may be
  omitted or soy powder
  substituted)
1 cup peanuts
1 cup sultanas
1 cup raisins
1 cup chopped dates

Heat the oil, peanut butter and honey together in a saucepan. Meanwhile, mix the remaining ingredients in a large bowl. Pour the hot mixture over the dry goodies and mix well.

Spread the resulting paste in a baking dish and bake in a moderately slow oven (160°C/325°F) for about 1 hour, stirring several times. When cool, store in an airtight container.

To make this more economical, when serving it up put one-sixth to one-quarter of a serve of raw rolled oats into each bowl and mix with the cooked muesli.

FAMILY MUESLI 149.

This is a fairly economical muesli. If you want to add other chopped dried fruit to it, do so, but it is quite nice like this. The recipe is for a very large quantity.

350 g honey
2½ cups oil
1 teaspoon sea salt
1 cup natural sultanas
3 cups nuts (any sort or all sorts
  — peanuts are the cheapest, of
  course)

½ cup sesame seeds
½ cup rye flakes
1 cup shredded coconut
1 cup lecithin granules
1 cup rice bran
16 cups rolled oats

Place a medium-sized saucepan on the kitchen scales and weigh in the honey. Then add the oil and salt and heat.

Meanwhile, mix the dry ingredients well in a very large bowl or half and half in two bowls.

When the honey and oil are frothy, quickly pour the liquid over the dry goodies and mix well.

Spread in two baking dishes and bake in a moderately low oven (160°C/325°F) for about 1 hour. Stir from time to time.

150. BUTTERY OATS FOR BREAKFAST

Serves 4-6

This is a delicious, but sinfully rich, way of serving oats for breakfast. It is good for times when the muesli has run out and no-one feels like porridge.

50 g butter (see Butter versus Margarine)	2 tablespoons honey
	2 tablespoons water
4 tablespoons oil	4 to 4½ cups rolled oats

Melt the butter, oil, honey and water together and, the minute they start bubbling, pour over the rolled oats and mix quickly.

Serve with fruit salad.

151. RAW BREAKFAST

If you are lucky enough to have access to raw milk, you must try it with raw oats. I know this doesn't sound too good, and it isn't if you have to use pasteurised milk, but if you can swamp a bowl of oats with raw milk and drizzle a spoonful of honey over it and then top that with fruit salad, or even just apples and strawberries in winter, the result is wonderful.

Also, if you are allergic to milk, you may find that raw milk can be handled by your body without a problem. Why? I think it's because the enzymes which are there to help digestion get killed by the pasteurisation heat, low as it may be.

But I must warn you to make sure your oats are nice and fresh. We were given raw oats by someone who ate porridge only rarely, and they were absolutely revolting, and then we found that another friend had a recently bought 'house' brand from a large supermarket chain, and it too was revolting, tasting just as bitter and nasty as the oats we knew to be stale.

Bibliography

Airola, P.: *Are You Confused?*, Health Plus Publishers, Phoenix, Arizona, 1971

Airola, P.: *Hypoglycemia: A Better Approach*, Health Plus Publishers, Phoenix, Arizona, 1977

Ashmead, D.: *Chelated Mineral Nutrition*, Institute Publishers, Huntinton Beach, California, 1981

Dufty, W.: *Sugar Blues*, Chilton, New York, 1975

Fukuoka, M.: *The One Straw Revolution*, Rodale Press, Emmaus, Pennsylvania, 1978

Hauschka, R.: *Nutrition*, Rudolf Steiner Press, London, 1983

Horsley, J.: *Sugar-Free Cookbook*, Prism Press, Great Britain, 1983

Leroi, R.: *An Anthroposophical Approach to Cancer*, Mercury Press, Spring Valley, New York, 1982

Minchin, M.: *Food for Thought*, Alma Publications/George Allen & Unwin, Sydney, 1982

Rochlitz, S.: *A New Form of Brain Hemisphere Repatterning; The Candida-Acetaldehyde, Formaldehyde and Cryptocides Hypothesis; New Postulates of Healing*, International Touch for Health Journal, U.S.A., 1985

Szekely, E.B.: *The Essene Gospel of Peace*, International Biogenic Society, U.S.A., 1981

Index